365
Quilt Blocks
a Year

Nancy J. Martin

Martingale
& COMPANY

Bothell, Washington

CREDITS

President	Nancy J. Martin
CEO/Publisher	Daniel J. Martin
Associate Publisher	Jane Hamada
Editorial Director	Mary V. Green
Design and Production Manager	Cheryl Stevenson
Cover Designer	Stan Green
Text Designer	Laurel Strand
Technical Editor	Ursula Reikes
Copy Editor	Liz McGehee
Illustrator	Laurel Strand

Martingale & COMPANY

That Patchwork Place

365 Quilts Blocks a Year
© 1999 by Nancy J. Martin
Martingale & Company
PO Box 118
Bothell, WA 98041-0118 USA

Printed in China

04 03 02 01 00 99   6 5 4 3 2 1

MISSION STATEMENT

We are dedicated to providing quality products
and service by working together to inspire creativity
and to enrich the lives we touch.

Basic Instructions

Cutting instructions are geared for rotary cutting. Quick-cutting techniques sometimes yield more pieces than needed; save any extras for another project. All measurements for block pieces include ¼"-wide seam allowances. Do not add seam allowances to the dimensions given in the cutting charts.

For triangles, cutting dimensions are provided for the square from which you'll cut half- or quarter-square triangles. When you see this symbol ◻, cut the square once diagonally to yield 2 half-square triangles. When you see this symbol ◻, cut the square twice diagonally to yield 4 quarter-square triangles.

Some odd-sized pieces are difficult to rotary cut. For those pieces, we have supplied piecing templates and trimming templates. Carefully trace the template onto stiff, clear plastic and cut out the shape.

To use a piecing template (indicated by PT in the charts), place the template right side up on the right side of the fabric. Trace around the template with a pencil and cut with scissors or align a rotary ruler with the edges of the template and rotary cut. To cut a reverse template (r), turn the template over so the wrong side of the template is face up before placing it on the right side of the fabric and cutting.

Trimming templates are indicated by TT in the charts. Cut the required-size squares or rectangles listed in the chart. The chart also indicates which corner(s) to trim. Place the trimming template in one corner, aligning the two straight sides of the trimming template with the outside edges of the squares or rectangles. Place a rotary ruler against the diagonal edge of the template: the plastic will stop the ruler at the proper position. Move the trimming template out of the way and cut along the ruler to remove the corner. Repeat for other corners if instructed to do so.

A quick way to cut and piece the smaller half-square triangles found in many of the blocks is to use the bias-square method. Cut two 8" squares of fabric and place them right sides together. Cut once diagonally, then cut strips in the width indicated in the chart below for the desired size of bias square.

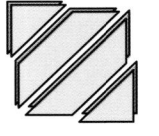

 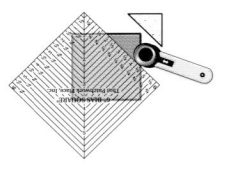

Push ruler against edge of trimming template.

Remove trimming template and cut along ruler.

Size of Half-Square Triangle	Finished Size of Triangle	Cut Size of Bias Square	Strip Width
1 3/8"	1 1/2"	2" x 2"	2"
2 3/8"	2"	2 1/2" x 2 1/2"	2 1/2"
3 3/8"	2 1/2"	3" x 3"	2 3/4"

Stitch the strips together to make two pieced squares. Using a bias square ruler, align the diagonal line of the ruler on the seam line and cut four bias squares from each piece.

Once you've cut all the pieces for a block it's time to put them together. Look for the most logical order in which to sew the pieces together. Whenever possible, sew the pieces together in rows, then join the rows as shown below.

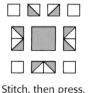

Stitch, then press.   Join units together.

Some blocks, however, cannot be sewn in straight rows. Instead, look for ways to join pieces into manageable units that can then be sewn together. In the block shown below, join the pieces that make up the center unit first, then join the pieces to make the triangle units. To complete the block, sew the triangle units to the center square.

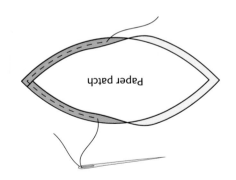

Several of the blocks are appliquéd or have appliqué accents. Appliqué templates are indicated with an AT. Use the paper-patch technique for appliqué.

1. Make a template out of plastic template material or lightweight cardboard for each appliqué pattern in the block. Do not add seam allowances to the templates.

2. Trace around the template shape on bond paper or freezer paper. Cut out the paper patch.

3. Pin or iron each paper patch to the wrong side of the fabric. If using freezer paper, pin with the plastic-coated side facing out.

4. Cut out each fabric shape, adding a ¼"-wide seam allowance all around.

5. With your fingers, turn the seam allowance over the edge of the paper patch and baste to the paper.

6. Press the appliqué pieces. Position, pin in place, and appliqué the pieces to the background fabric in numerical order.

Paper patch

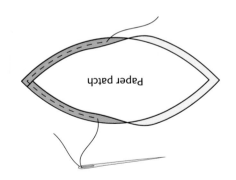

9

Bias appliqué is used on several of the blocks. These are indicated on the block diagrams in blue.

1. Cut each bias strip 1" wide and long enough for the individual appliqué (plus a couple extra inches for insurance). For the teapot (March 3), cut bias strips 1½" wide.

2. Fold the bias strip in half, wrong sides together, and stitch ⅛" from the edges. Press into a tube so the seam falls in the middle of the back.

3. Place the bias tube on the background fabric, forming the desired shape. Pin and stitch in place.

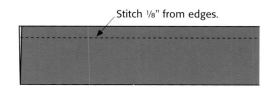

Stitch ⅛" from edges.

Back of tube

To stitch the appliqués, use a single strand of thread that matches the appliqué pieces.

1. Start the first stitch from the wrong side of the background fabric. Bring the needle up through the background fabric and through the folded edge of the appliqué piece.

2. Insert the needle next to where you brought it up, but this time go through the background fabric only.

3. Bring the needle up through the background fabric and into the folded edge of the appliqué piece, catching 1 or 2 threads. Space your stitches a little less than 1/8" apart.

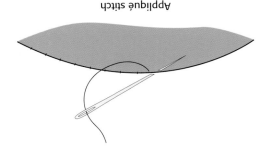

Appliqué stitch

4. For larger shapes, slit the background fabric when the appliqué is complete and pull out the paper patch.

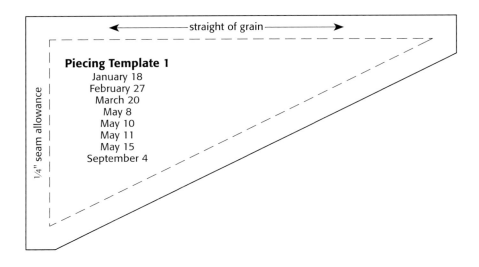

straight of grain

Piecing Template 1
January 18
February 27
March 20
May 8
May 10
May 11
May 15
September 4

¼" seam allowance

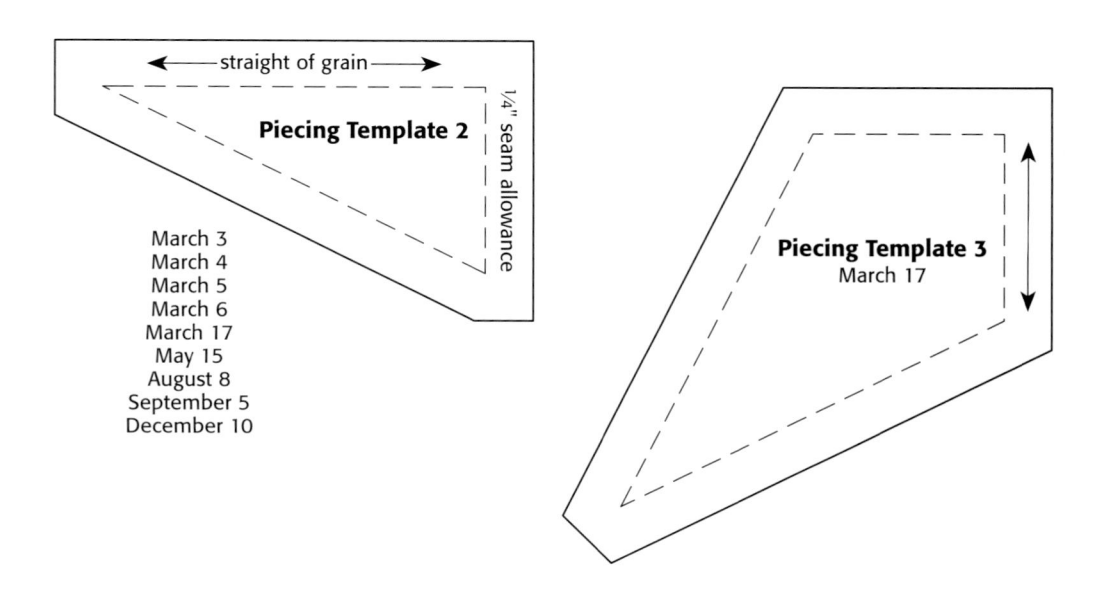

straight of grain

Piecing Template 2

¼" seam allowance

March 3
March 4
March 5
March 6
March 17
May 15
August 8
September 5
December 10

Piecing Template 3
March 17

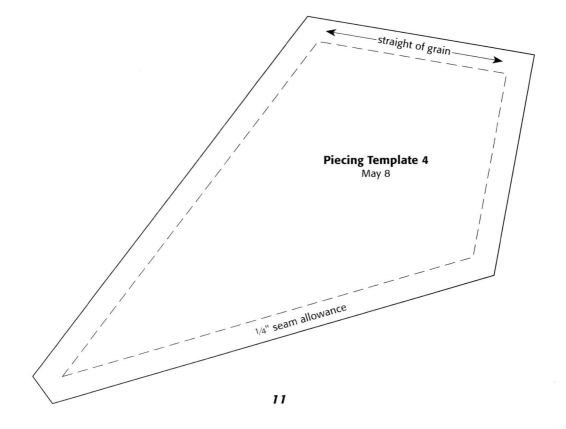

Piecing Template 4
May 8

straight of grain

1/4" seam allowance

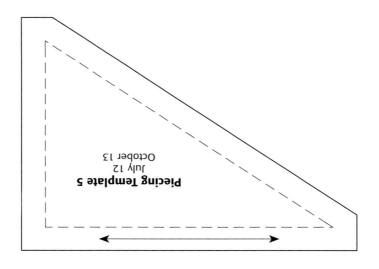

Piecing Template 5
July 12
October 13

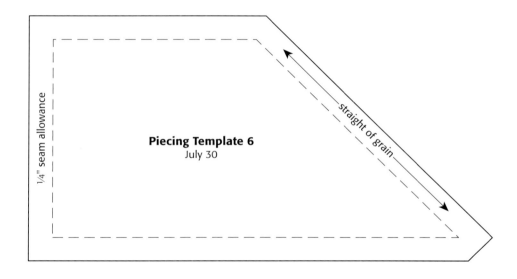

Piecing Template 6
July 30

¼" seam allowance

straight of grain

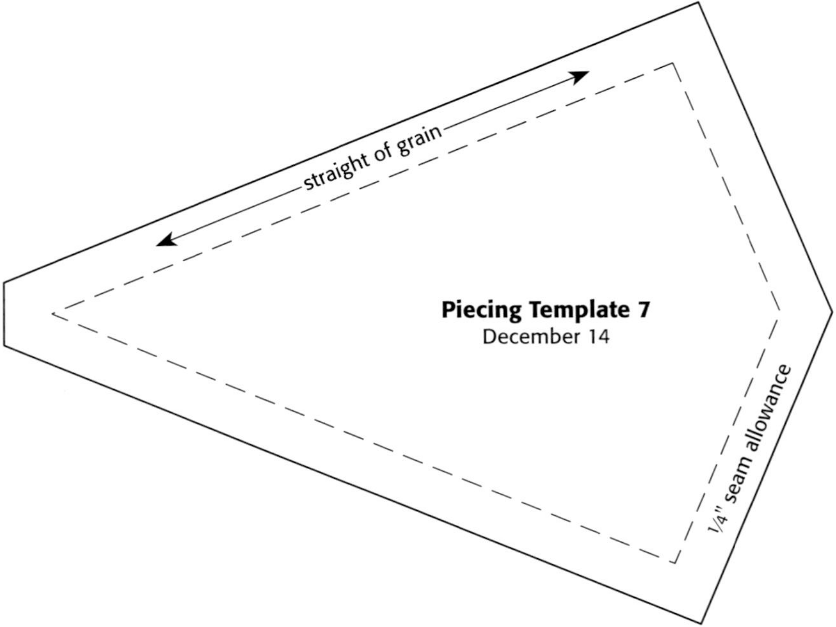

¼" seam allowance

Piecing Template 7
December 14

straight of grain

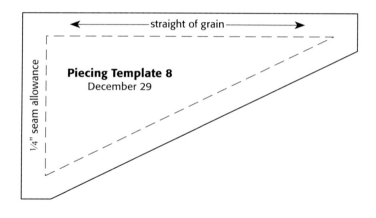

straight of grain

¼" seam allowance

Piecing Template 8
December 29

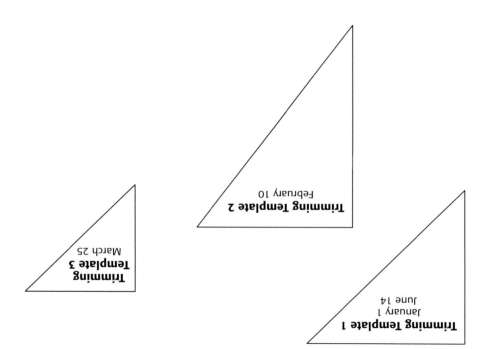

Trimming Template 1
January 1
June 14

Trimming Template 2
February 10

Trimming Template 3
March 25

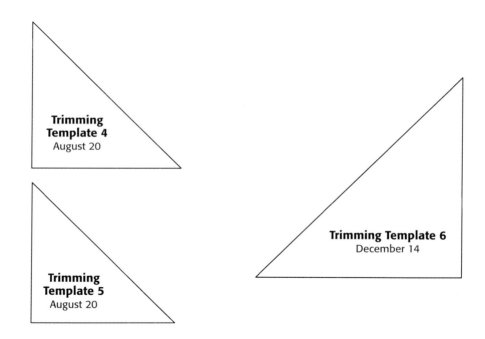

Trimming Template 4
August 20

Trimming Template 5
August 20

Trimming Template 6
December 14

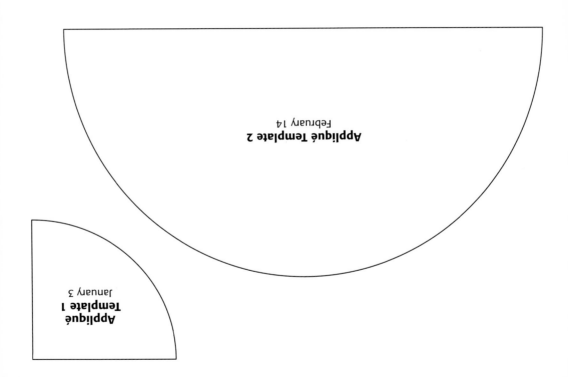

Appliqué Template 2
February 14

Appliqué Template 1
January 3

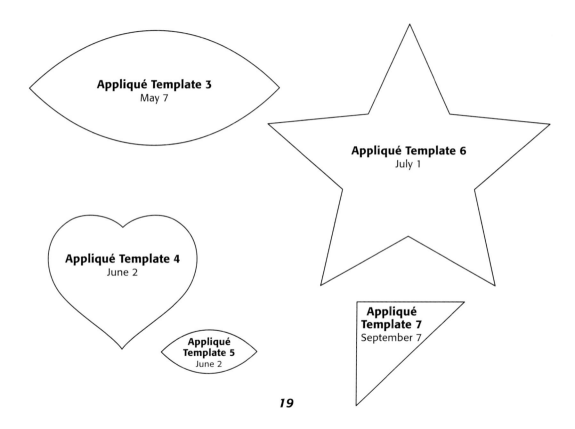

Appliqué Template 3
May 7

Appliqué Template 6
July 1

Appliqué Template 4
June 2

Appliqué Template 5
June 2

Appliqué Template 7
September 7

19

Appliqué Templates
Sunbonnet Sue
August 13

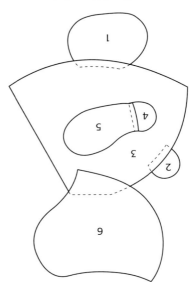

Appliqué Templates
Overall Bill
August 14

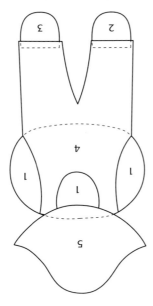

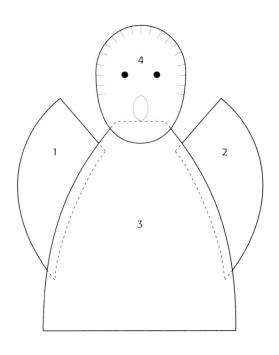

Appliqué Templates
Angelsong
December 5

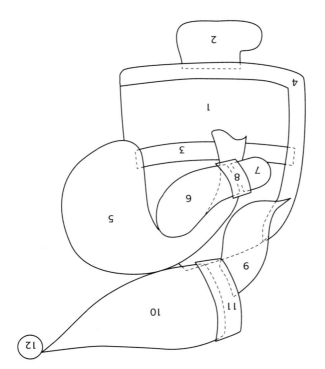

Appliqué Templates
Here Comes Santa Claus
December 9

Winter
January-March

For quilters, there's no better time than the chilly winter months to cozy up indoors and quilt, quilt, quilt! Along with traditional favorites for January, you'll find blocks depicting the central themes of a quilter's winter: snowing and sewing. Friends and loved ones will delight in February's block patterns, which include romantic hearts and friendship blocks for Valentine's Day, as well as patriotic designs to honor Presidents' Day. During March, choose from blocks that feature the month's infamous winds and other themes, such as tea parties, dishes, St. Patrick's Day, and the first day of spring.

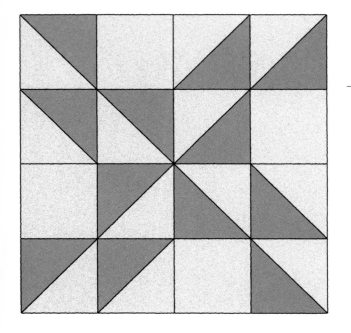

DECEMBER
31

Year's Favorite
8"

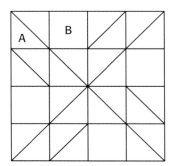

A ◻ 2⅞"   B ☐ 2½"

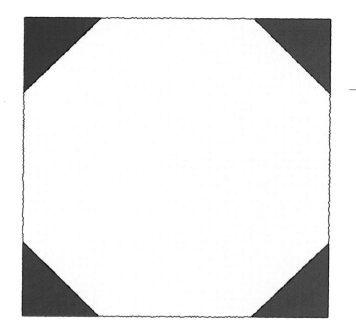

JANUARY
1

Snowball
6"

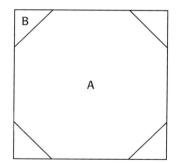

A ⬜ 6½" / TT-1   B ◻ 2⅜"

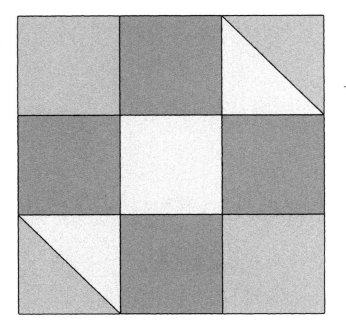

DECEMBER
30

Hour Glass
9"

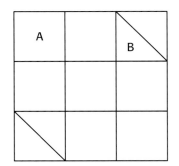

A [] 3½"   B [/] 3⅞"

JANUARY

2

Snowflake
12"

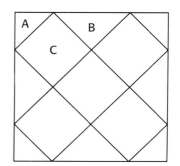

A ⬚ 3⅞"   B ⧇ 7¼"   C ▢ 4¾"

Resolutions
13½"

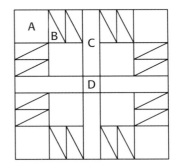

A ☐ 3½"   B ◺ PT-8   C ▭ 2" × 6½"   D ☐ 2"

JANUARY
3

Snowy Windows
8"

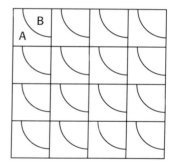

A ☐ 2½"   B ◗ AT-1

DECEMBER
28

Three Steps
12"

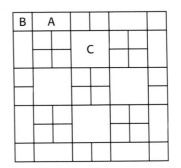

A ☐ 2" × 3½"   B ☐ 2"   C ☐ 3½"

JANUARY
4

Snow Crystals
16"

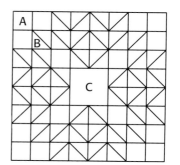

A ☐ 2½"   B ◻ 2⅞"   C ☐ 4½"

DECEMBER
27

Balance
15"

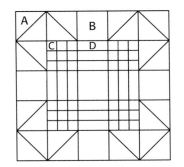

A ◳ 3⅞" B ☐ 3½" C ☐ 1½" D ☐ 1½" × 3½"

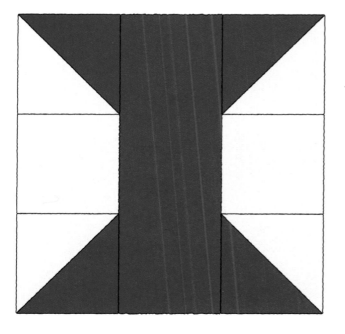

JANUARY
5

Spools
6"

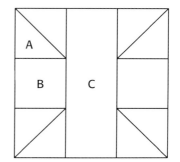

A ▱ 2⅞"   B ☐ 2½"   C ▭ 2½" × 6½"

DECEMBER
26

Providence
10"

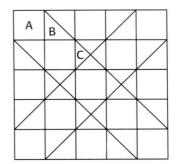

A ☐ 2½"   B ◩ 2⅞"   C ⊠ 3¼"

JANUARY
6

Chimney Sweep
10½"

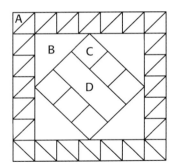

A ◺ 2⅜"   B ◺ 4⅝"   C ☐ 2¼"   D ☐ 2¼" × 5¾"

DECEMBER
25

Star of Bethlehem
12"

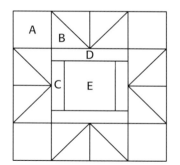

A   3½"   B ◿ 3⅞"   C ▭ 1½" × 4½"   D ▭ 1½" × 6½"   E ▭ 4½"

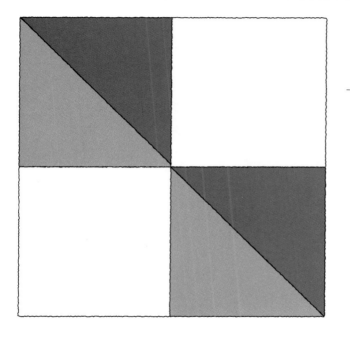

JANUARY
7

Cotton Reels
8"

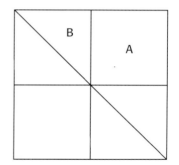

A ☐ 4½" B ◩ 4⅞"

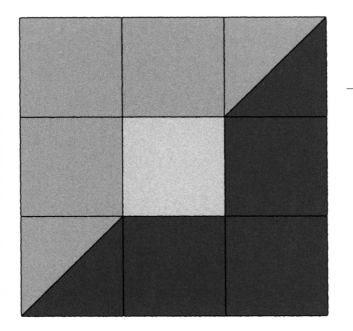

DECEMBER
24

Nine Patch Variation
9"

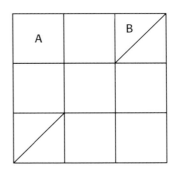

A ☐ 3½"   B ◺ 3⅞"

JANUARY
8

Flying Shuttles
12"

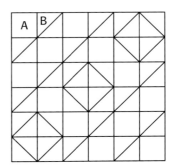

A ☐ 2½"   B ◩ 2⅞"

DECEMBER
23

Christmas Cracker
8"

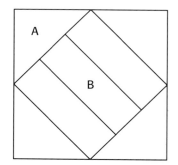

A ◹ 4⅞"   B ▭ 2⅜" × 6⅛"

JANUARY
9

Spool and Bobbin
8"

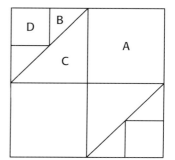

A ☐ 4½"   B ◿ 2⅞"   C ◿ 4⅞"   D ☐ 2½"

DECEMBER
22

Rising Star
12"

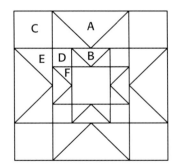

A ⊠ 7¼"   B ⊠ 4¼"   C ☐ 3½"   D ☐ 2"   E ◩ 3⅞"   F ◩ 2⅜"

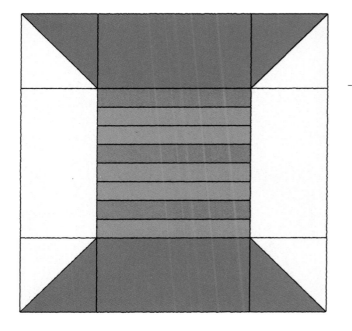

JANUARY
10

Spool of Thread
8"

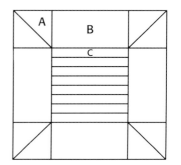

A | B
C

A ◻ 2⅞"   B ▭ 2½" × 4½"   C ▭ 1" × 4½"

Christmas Basket
8"

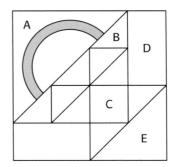

A ▱ 6⅞"   B ▱ 2⅞"   C ☐ 2½"   D ▭ 2½" × 4½"   E ▱ 4⅞"

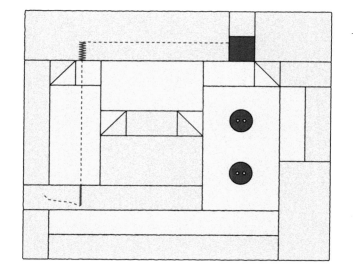

JANUARY
11

Sew and Sew
10" x 12"

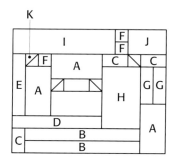

A ⬜ 2½" × 4½"

B ⬜ 1½" × 9½"

C ⬜ 1½" × 2½"

D ⬜ 1½" × 7½"

E ⬜ 1½" × 5½"

F ⬜ 1½"

G ⬜ 1½" × 3½"

H ⬜ 3½" × 5½"

I ⬜ 2½" × 8½"

J ⬜ 2½" × 3½"

K ◩ 1⅞"

Embroider details.

DECEMBER
20

Fireside Visitor
9"

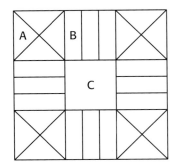

A ⊠ 4¼"   B ▭ 1½" × 3½"   C ☐ 3½"

JANUARY
12

Beginner's Delight
10"

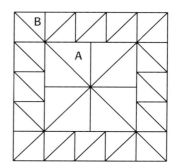

A ⊿ 3⅞"   B ⊿ 2⅞"

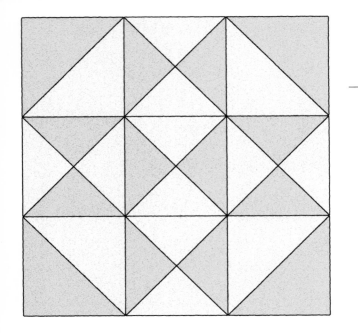

DECEMBER
19

Silent Star
9"

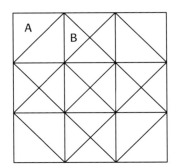

A ◹ 3⅞"   B ⊠ 4¼"

JANUARY
13

Handy Andy
10"

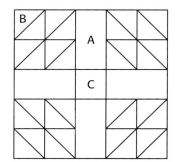

A ▢ 2½" × 4½"   B ◩ 2⅞"   C ▢ 2½"

DECEMBER
18

Starry Path
10"

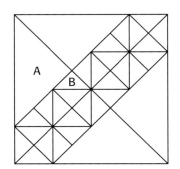

A ⊠ 8¾"   B ⊠ 3¾"

JANUARY
14

Rambler
10"

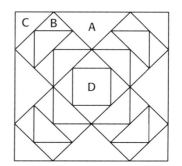

A ⊠ 6¼"   B ⊠ 3¾"   C ◹ 3⅜"   D ☐ 3"

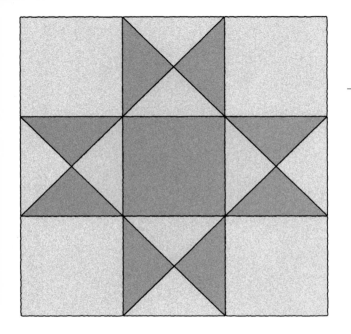

DECEMBER
17

Star of Hope
9"

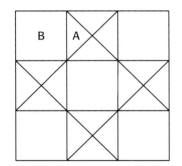

A ⊠ 4¼" B ☐ 3½"

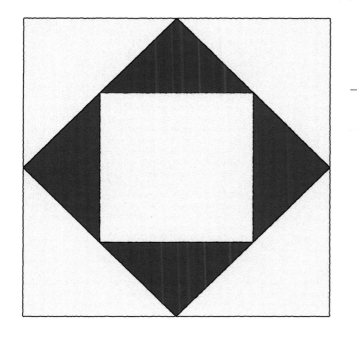

JANUARY
15

Economy
10"

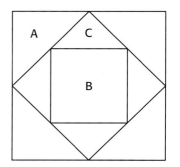

A ◸ 5⅞" B ☐ 5½" C ⊠ 6¼"

DECEMBER
16

Eight Hands Around
12"

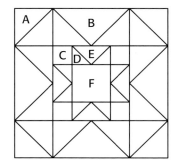

A ◲ 3⅞"   C ☐ 2"   E ⊠ 4¼"
B ⊠ 7¼"   D ◲ 2⅜"   F ☐ 3½"

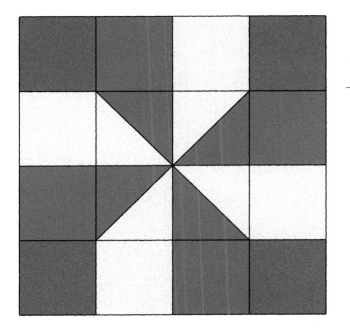

JANUARY
16

Nelson's Victory
8"

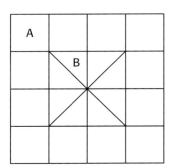

A ☐ 2½"   B ◻ 2⅞"

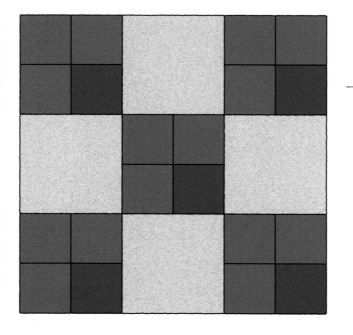

Puss in the Corner
12"

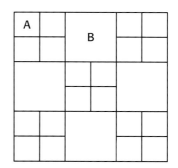

A ☐ 2½"   B ☐ 4½"

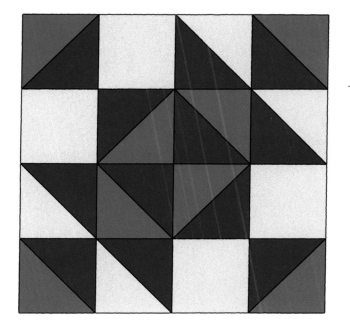

JANUARY
17

Flying Dutchman
10"

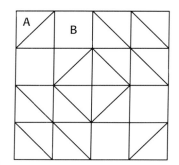

A ◹ 3⅜"   B ☐ 3"

Twinkling Star
12"

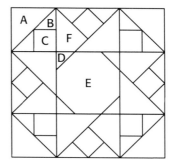

A ◩ 4⅜" B ◩ 2⅝" C ☐ 2¼" D ◩ 2⅞" E ⬚ 5½" / TT-6 F △ PT-7

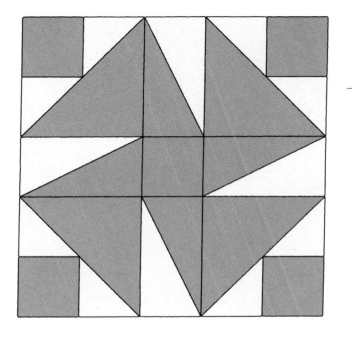

JANUARY
18

Crazy Ann
10"

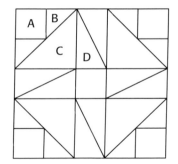

A ☐ 2½" B ◩ 2⅞" C ◩ 4⅞" D ◺ PT-1

DECEMBER
13

Bright Star
12"

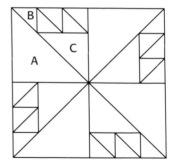

A ◻ 6⅞"   B ◻ 2⅞"   C ◻ 4⅞"

JANUARY
19

Aunt Dinah
9"

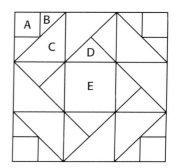

A ☐ 2"   B ◸ 2⅜"   C ◸ 3⅞"   D ⊠ 4¼"   E ☐ 3½"

DECEMBER
12

Tennessee Pine
12"

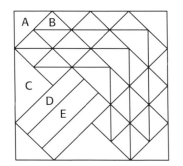

A ◻ 3⅞" B ⊠ 4¼" C ⊠ 7¼" D ▭ 1⅞" × 6⅞" E ▭ 2" × 6⅞"

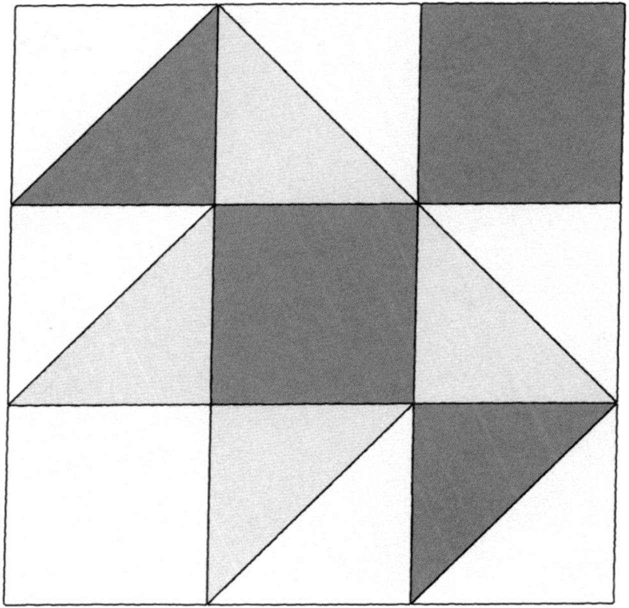

JANUARY
20

Darting Birds
6"

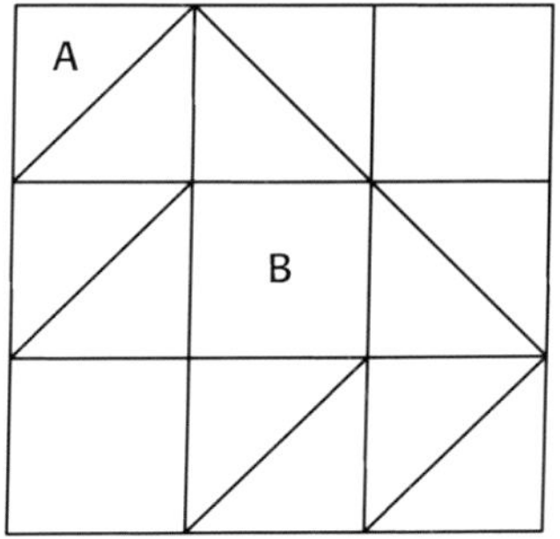

A ◪ 2⅞"   B □ 2½"

DECEMBER
11

Proud Pine
12"

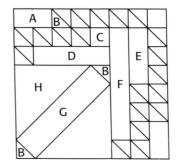

A ▭ 2" × 3½" D ▭ 2" × 6½" G ▭ 2⅝" × 9"
B ◪ 2⅜" E ▭ 2" × 5" H ◪ 6⅞"
C ▢ 2" F ▭ 2" × 9½"

JANUARY
21

Double Cross
10"

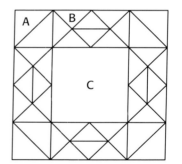

A 3⅜"   B ⊠ 3¾"   C ☐ 5½"

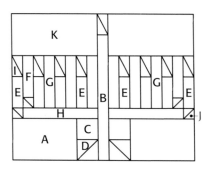

DECEMBER
10

Menorah
14" x 17"

A ⬜ 4½" × 6½"
B ⬜ 1½" × 12½"
C ⬜ 2½"
D ◩ 2⅞"
E ⬜ 1½" × 3½"
F ⬜ 1½" × 4½"
G ⬜ 1½" × 5½"
H ⬜ 1½" × 7½"
I ◺ PT-2 reversed
J ◩ 1⅞"
K ⬜ 4½" × 8½"

JANUARY
22

Evening Star
9"

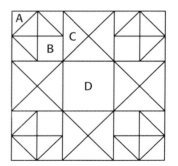

A ◹ 2³⁄₈"   B ☐ 2"   C ⊠ 4¹⁄₄"   D ☐ 3¹⁄₂"

DECEMBER
9

Here Comes Santa Claus
6"

A ☐ 6½"

Appliqué templates on page 22.

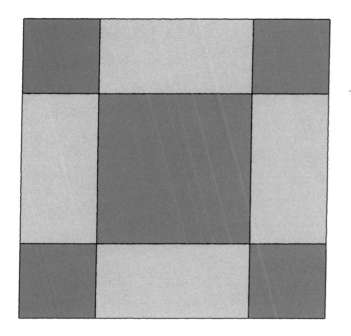

JANUARY
23

Puss in a Corner
7½"

A	B	
	C	

A ☐ 2¼" B ▭ 2¼" × 4½" C ☐ 4½"

DECEMBER
8

Christmas Wreath
7" x 11"

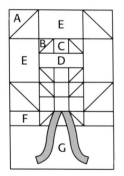

A ▨ 2⅞" C ☐ 1½"   E ☐ 2½" × 3½"   G ☐ 3½" × 7½"
B ▨ 1⅞" D ☐ 1½" × 3½" F ☐ 1½" × 2½"

JANUARY
24

Old Favorite
12"

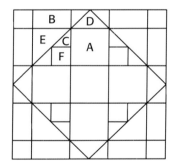

A ☐ 3½" C ◩ 2⅜" E ◩ 3⅞"

B ☐ 2" × 3½" D ⊠ 4¼" F ☐ 2"

DECEMBER
7

Star-Crossed Christmas
13½"

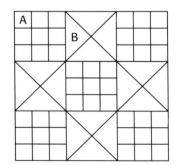

A □ 2"   B ⊠ 5¾"

JANUARY
25

Four Corners
9"

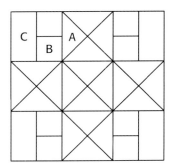

A ⊠ 4¼"   B ☐ 2"   C ▭ 2" × 3½"

DECEMBER
6

Ribbon Block
14"

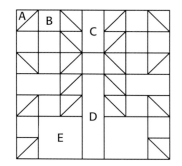

A ◻ 2⅞"   B ☐ 2½"   C ▭ 2½" × 4½"   D ▭ 2½" × 8½"   E ☐ 4½"

JANUARY
26

Chinese Puzzle
10"

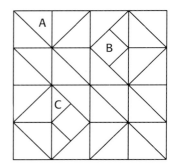

A ◹ 3⅜"   B ☐ 2¼"   C ⊠ 3¾"

DECEMBER
5

Angelsong
5" x 6"

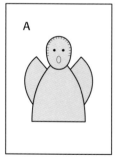

A

A ☐ 5½" × 6½"

Embroider face and hair.
Appliqué templates on page 21.

JANUARY
27

Telephone
12"

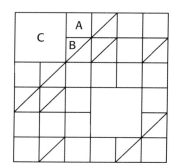

A ☐ 2½"   B ◸ 2⅞"   C ☐ 4½"

DECEMBER
4

Friendship Star
12"

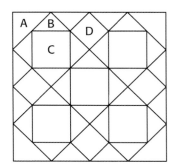

A ◻ 3⅞"   B ⊠ 4¼"   C ☐ 3½"   D ☐ 2⅝"

JANUARY
28

Castles in the Air
9"

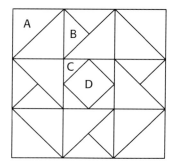

A ◻ 3⅞"   B ⊠ 4¼"   C ◻ 2⅜"   D ☐ 2⅝"

DECEMBER
3

Christmas Tree
12"

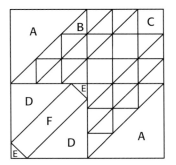

A ◹ 6⅞" C ☐ 2½" E ◹ 2⅛"
B ◹ 2⅞" D ◹ 5⅝" F ☐ 2¼" × 7¼"

JANUARY
29

City Streets
9"

A	B	C		
		D		
		E		

A ☐ 2½" B ☐ 1½" × 2½" C ☐ 2½" × 3½" D ☐ 1½" × 3½" E ☐ 3½"

DECEMBER
2

Tree of Life
12"

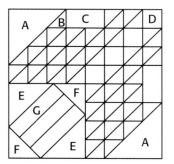

A ▱ 5⅜" C ▭ 2" × 3½" E ◺ 4⅜" G ▭ 1¹¹⁄₁₆" × 5½"

B ◿ 2⅜" D ▯ 2" F ◺ 3⅜"

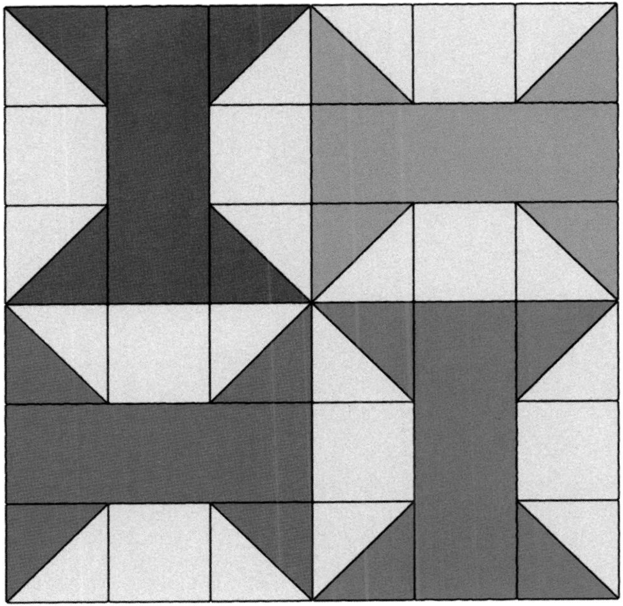

JANUARY
30

Borrow and Lend
12"

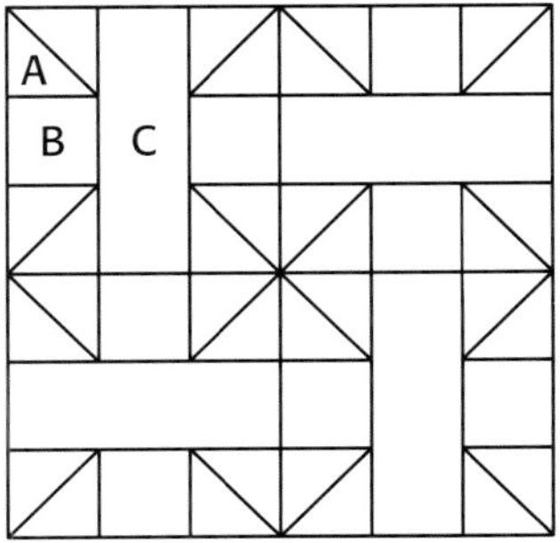

A 2 7/8"   B 2 1/2"   C 2 1/2" × 6 1/2"

Pine Tree
10"

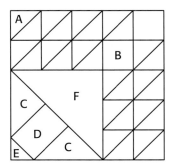

A ◻ 2⅞"   B ☐ 2½"   C ⊠ 5¾"   D ▭ 2⅝" × 3¹¹⁄₁₆"   E ◻ 2⅜"   F ◻ 6⅞"

JANUARY
31

Oklahoma Boomer
6"

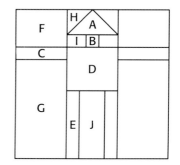

A ⊠ 3¼"
B ☐ 1"
C ☐ 1" × 2½"
D ☐ 2¼" × 2½"
E ☐ 1" × 3¼"
F ☐ 2" × 2½"
G ☐ 2½" × 4½"
H ◺ 1⅞"
I ☐ 1" × 1¼"
J ☐ 1½" × 3¼"

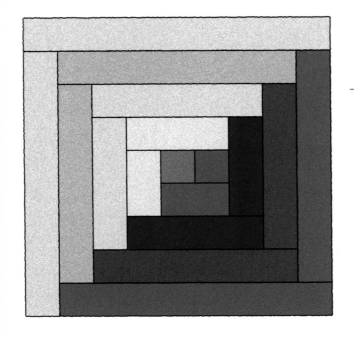

Log Cabin
9"

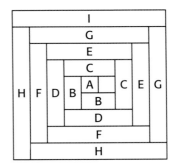

A ☐ 1½"

B ☐ 1½" × 2½"

C ☐ 1½" × 3½"

D ☐ 1½" × 4½"

E ☐ 1½" × 5½"

F ☐ 1½" × 6½"

G ☐ 1½" × 7½"

H ☐ 1½" × 8½"

I ☐ 1½" × 9½"

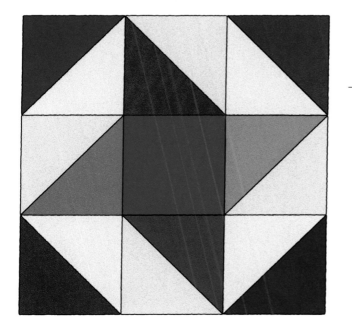

FEBRUARY
1

Friendship Star
6"

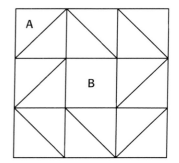

A ◹ 2⅞"   B ☐ 2½"

NOVEMBER
29

Harvest Basket
10"

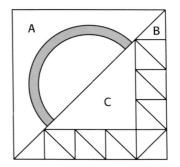

A ◹ 10⅞"   B ◹ 2⅞"   C ◹ 6⅞"

FEBRUARY
2

Hand of Friendship
14"

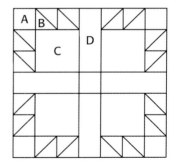

A ☐ 2½"   B ◩ 2⅞"   C ☐ 4½"   D ▭ 2½" × 6½"

NOVEMBER
28

Four Knaves
10"

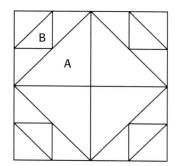

A ◻ 5⅞"   B ◻ 3⅜"

FEBRUARY
3

Album
9"

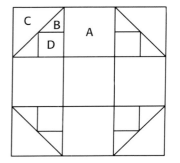

A ☐ 3½" B ◩ 2⅜" C ◩ 3⅞" D ☐ 2"

NOVEMBER
27

Leavenworth Nine Patch
10½"

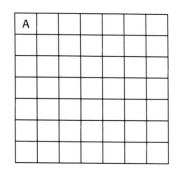

A ☐ 2"

FEBRUARY
4

Album Patch
15"

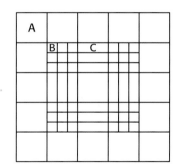

A ☐ 3½" B ☐ 1½" C ☐ 1½" × 3½"

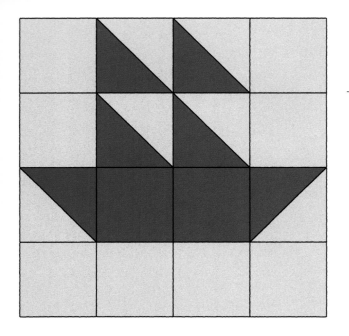

NOVEMBER
26

Mayflower
8"

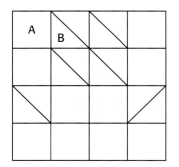

A ☐ 2½"   B ◩ 2⅞"

FEBRUARY
5

Best Friend
14"

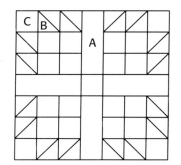

A ⬜ 2½" × 6½"   B ◩ 2⅞"   C ⬜ 2½"

NOVEMBER
25

Turkey Tracks
9"

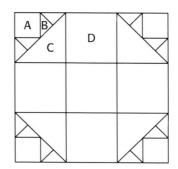

A ☐ 2" B ☒ 2¾" C ◺ 3⅞" D ☐ 3½"

FEBRUARY
6

Next Door Neighbor
8"

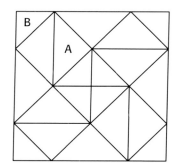

A ⊠ 5¼"   B ◻ 2⅞"

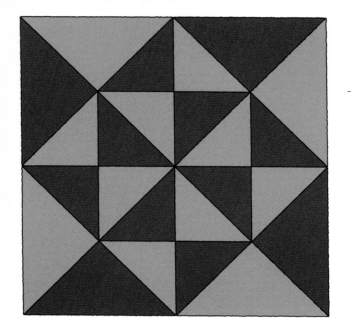

NOVEMBER
24

Peace and Plenty
9"

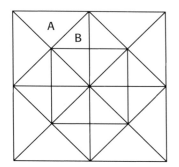

A ⊠ 5¾"   B ◺ 3⅛"

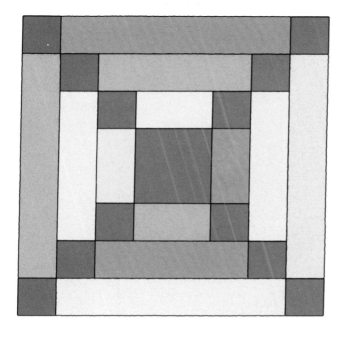

FEBRUARY
7

Chimneys and Cornerstones
8"

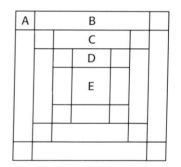

A ☐ 1½"   B ☐ 1½" × 6½"   C ☐ 1½" × 4½"   D ☐ 1½" × 2½"   E ☐ 2½"

NOVEMBER
23

Spinning Arrows
12"

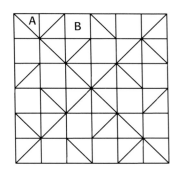

A ◩ 2⅞"   B ☐ 2½"

FEBRUARY
8

Kansas Troubles
16"

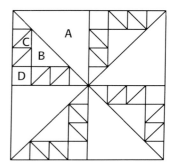

A ◹ 8⅞"   B ◹ 4⅞"   C ◹ 2⅞"   D ☐ 2½"

NOVEMBER
22

Indian Mats
12"

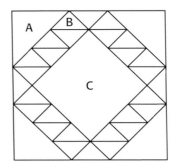

A ◸ 5⅜"   B ◿ 3"   C ☐ 6⅞"

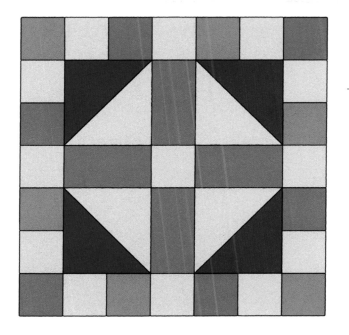

FEBRUARY
9

Lincoln's Platform
10½"

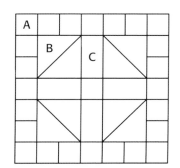

A ☐ 2"   B ◻ 3⅞"   C ☐ 2" × 3½"

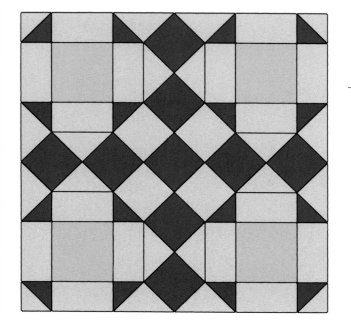

NOVEMBER
21

Indian Squares
10"

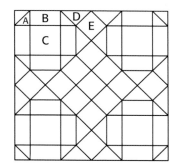

A ◻ 1⅞"   B ▭ 1½" × 2½"   C ▢ 2½"   D ◻ 3¼"   E ▢ 1¹⁵⁄₁₆"

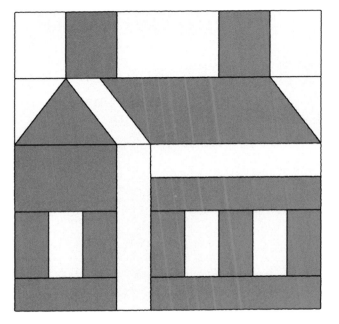

FEBRUARY
10

Lincoln's Cabin Home
9"

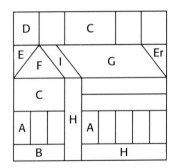

A ▭ 1½" × 2½"

B ▭ 1½" × 3½"

C ▭ 2½" × 3½"

D ▭ 2" × 2½"

E ◹ 2" × 2½" / TT-2

Er ◸ 2" × 2½" / TT-2 rev.

F ◺ 2½" × 3½" / TT-2

G ◹ 2½" × 8" / TT-2

H ▭ 1½" × 5½"

I ◹ 2½" × 3" / TT-2

NOVEMBER
20

Indian Maze
12"

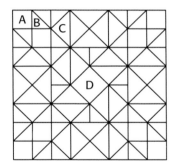

A ☐ 2" B ◹ 2⅜" C ⊠ 4¼" D ☐ 2⅝"

FEBRUARY
11

Underground Railroad
12"

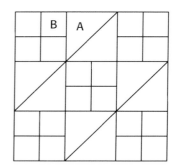

A ◩ 4⅞"   B ☐ 2½"

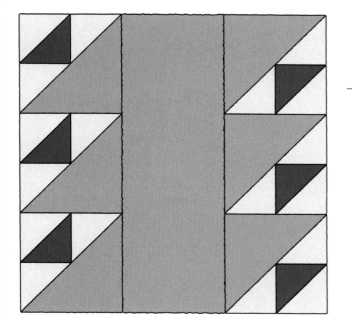

NOVEMBER
19

Wampum
9"

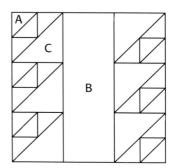

A ◹ 2³⁄₈" B ▭ 3¹⁄₂" × 9¹⁄₂" C ◹ 3⁷⁄₈"

FEBRUARY
12

Rail Fence
12"

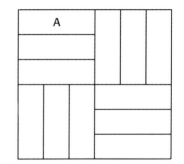

A ▭ 2½" × 6½"

NOVEMBER
18

Indian
10"

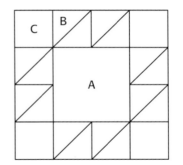

A ☐ 5½"   B ◹ 3⅜"   C ☐ 3"

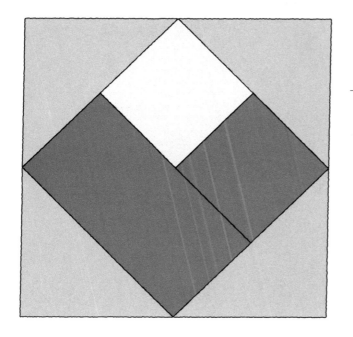

Log Cabin Heart
4¼"

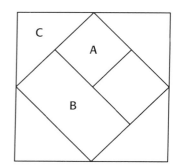

A ☐ 2"   B ⬭ 2" × 3½"   C ◪ 3"

Indian Plume
12"

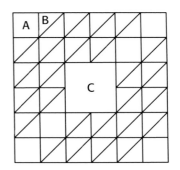

A ☐ 2½"   B ◪ 2⅞"   C ☐ 4½"

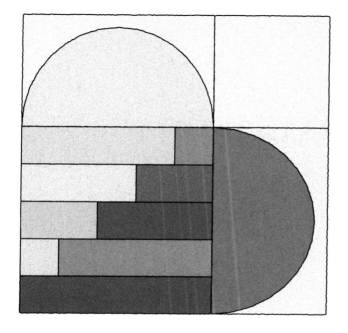

FEBRUARY
14

Be My Valentine
8"

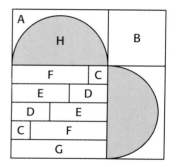

A ☐ 3½" × 5½"

B ☐ 3½"

C ☐ 1½"

D ☐ 1½" × 2½"

E ☐ 1½" × 3½"

F ☐ 1½" × 4½"

G ☐ 1½" × 5½"

H ◠ AT-2

NOVEMBER
16

Arrow Crown
12"

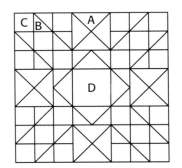

A ◻ 4¼"   B ◹ 2⅜"   C ☐ 2"   D ☐ 3½"

FEBRUARY
15

Watercolor Heart
6"

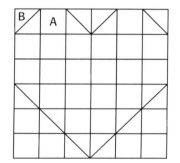

A ☐ 1½"   B ◩ 1⅞"

NOVEMBER
15

Indian Trails
12"

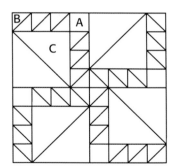

A ☐ 2" B ◩ 2⅜" C ◩ 5⅜"

FEBRUARY
16

True Lover's Knot
14"

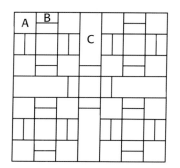

A ☐ 2½"   B ▭ 1½" × 2½"   C ▭ 2½" × 5½"

NOVEMBER
14

Bear's Paw
10½"

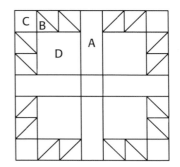

A ▭ 2" × 5"   B ◨ 2⅜"   C ▢ 2"   D ▢ 3½"

FEBRUARY
17

Chevron
9"

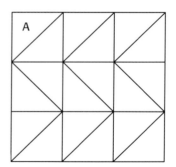

A ◻ 3⅞"

NOVEMBER
13

Airplane
12"

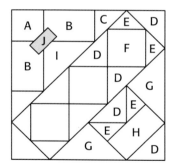

A ▢ 3"
B ▭ 3" × 4½"
C ◪ 3⅜"
D ◪ 3⅞"
E ◪ 3"
F ▢ 3½"
G ⊠ 7¼"
H ▭ 2⅝" × 4¾"
I ◪ 4⅞"

J ▭ 1½" × 2½" (appliqué)

FEBRUARY
18

Mosaic
8"

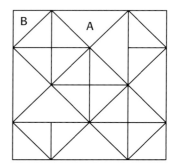

A ⊠ 5¼"   B ◻ 2⅞"

NOVEMBER
12

Aircraft
12"

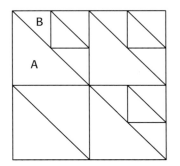

A ◹ 6⅞"   B ◹ 3⅞"

FEBRUARY
19

Mountain Homespun
9"

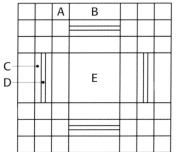

A ☐ 1½"   B ☐ 1½" × 3½"   C ☐ ⅞" × 3½"   D ☐ ¾" × 3½"   E ☐ 3½"

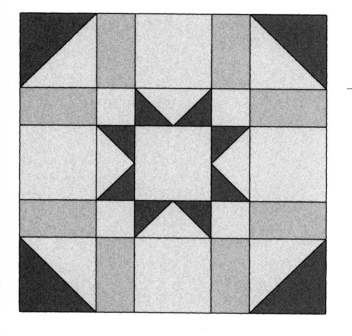

NOVEMBER
11

Army Star
12"

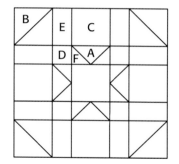

A ⊠ 4¼" B ◩ 3⅞" C ☐ 3½" D ☐ 2" E ▭ 2" × 3½" F ◩ 2⅜"

FEBRUARY
20

Texas Treasure
12"

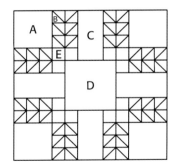

A ☐ 3½"   B ◩ 1⅞"   C ▭ 2½" × 4½"   D ☐ 4½"   E ☐ 1½"

NOVEMBER
10

Sargeant's Chevron
8"

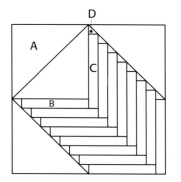

A ▨ 4⅞" B ▭ 1" × 4" C ▭ 1" × 4½" D ▧ 1⅜"

FEBRUARY
21

Cherry Tree
7½"

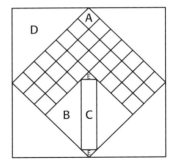

A ☐ 1¼"   B ◪ 3⅜"   C ▭ 1¼" × 4"   D ◪ 4⅝"   E ◪ 1⁷⁄₁₆"

NOVEMBER
9

Almanizer
12"

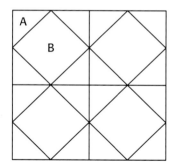

A ◩ 3⅞" B ☐ 4¾"

FEBRUARY
22

Washington's Elm
16"

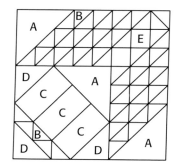

A ▱ 6⅞"   B ▱ 2⅞"   C ▭ 3⅜" × 6⅛"   D ▱ 4⅞"   E ▢ 2½"

NOVEMBER
8

Cross Roads
8"

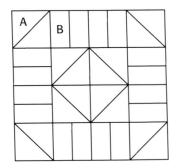

A ◧ 2⅞"   B ▭ 1½" × 2½"

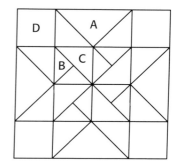

FEBRUARY
23

Martha Washington Star
8"

A ⊠ 5¼"   B ⊠ 3¼"   C ◩ 2⅞"   D ☐ 2½"

NOVEMBER
7

Squares Upon Squares
10"

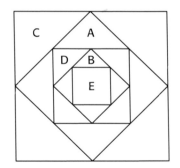

A ⊠ 6¼"   B ⊠ 3¾"   C ◩ 5⅞"   D ◩ 3⅜"   E ☐ 3"

Dolley Madison's Star
9"

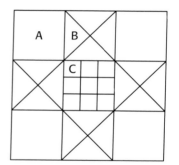

A ☐ 3½"   B ☒ 4¼"   C ☐ 1½"

NOVEMBER
6

Combination Star
9"

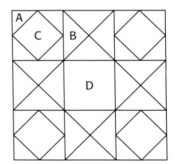

A ◹ 2⅜" B ⊠ 4¼" C ☐ 2⅝" D ☐ 3½"

FEBRUARY
25

Barbara Frietchie Star
12"

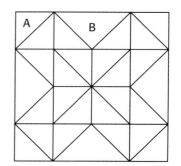

A ◹ 3⅞" B ◌ 7¼"

NOVEMBER
5

Cats and Mice
12"

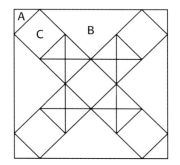

A ◹ 2⅞"   B ⊠ 9¼"   C ☐ 3⁵⁄₁₆"

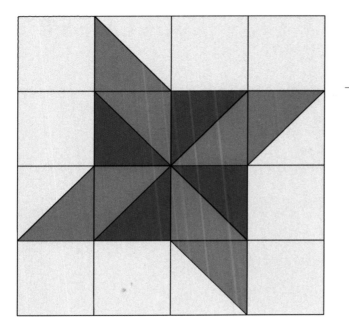

Clay's Choice
8"

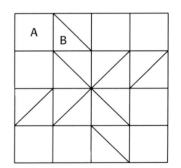

A ☐ 2½"   B ◻ 2⅞"

NOVEMBER
4

Lighthouse
10"

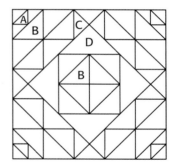

A ◻ 1⅞"   B ◻ 2⅞"   C ⊠ 3¼"   D ⊠ 5¼"

FEBRUARY
27

Fifty-four Forty or Fight
12"

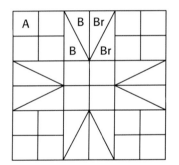

A ☐ 2½"   B ◤ PT-1   Br ◥ PT-1 reversed

NOVEMBER
3

Eddystone Light
9"

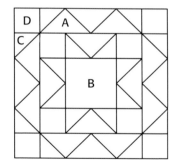

A ⊠ 4¼"   B ☐ 3½"   C ◩ 2³⁄₈"   D ☐ 2"

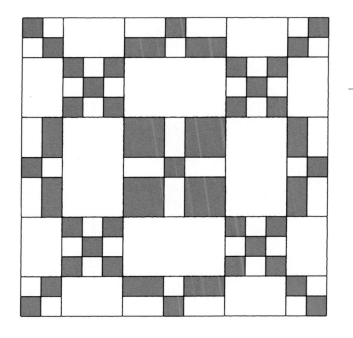

FEBRUARY
28

Burgoyne Surrounded
15"

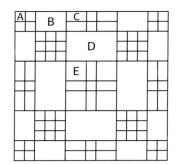

A ☐ 1½"   B ☐ 2½" × 3½"   C ☐ 1½" × 2½"   D ☐ 3½" × 5½"   E ☐ 2½"

Jack's Delight
9"

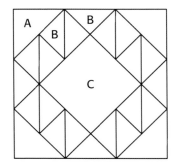

A ◻ 3⅞"   B ⊠ 4¼"   C ☐ 4¾"

FEBRUARY
29

Free Trade
10"

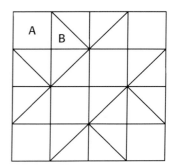

A ☐ 3"   B ◹ 3⅜"

NOVEMBER
1

Carrie Nation Quilt
8"

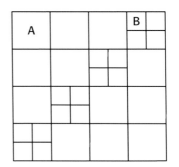

A ☐ 2½"   B ☐ 1½"

MARCH
1

Broken Dishes
10"

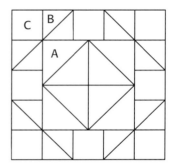

A ⟋ 3⅞"   B ⟋ 2⅞"   C ☐ 2½"

OCTOBER
31

BOO
15"

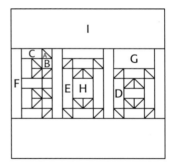

A ◩ 1⅞"

B ▢ 1½"

C ▭ 1½" × 2½"

D ▭ 1½" × 3½"

E ▭ 1½" × 4½"

F ▭ 1½" × 7½"

G ▭ 2½" × 4½"

H ▢ 2"

I ▭ 4½" × 15½"

MARCH
2

Cups and Saucers
9"

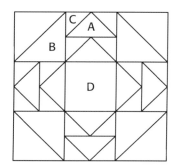

A ⊠ 4¼" B ◸ 3⅞" C ◸ 2⅜" D ☐ 3½"

OCTOBER
30

Jack-O-Lantern
10"

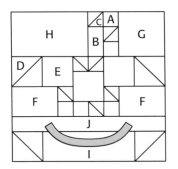

A ☐ 1½"

B ☐ 1½" × 2½"

C ◩ 1⅞"

D ◩ 2⅞"

E ☐ 2½"

F ☐ 2½" × 3½"

G ☐ 3½"

H ☐ 3½" × 5½"

I ☐ 2½" × 6½"

J ☐ 1½" × 10½"

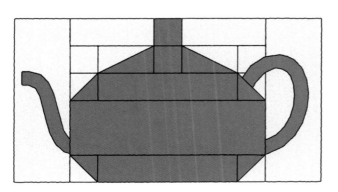

Teapot
11" x 6"

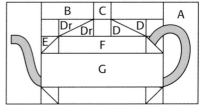

A ▢ 2½" × 6½" C ▢ 1½" Dr ◸ PT-2 reversed F ▢ 1½" × 5½"

B ▢ 1½" × 3½" D ◺ PT-2 E ▨ 1⅞" G ▢ 2½" × 7½"

OCTOBER
29

Gentlemen's Fancy
9"

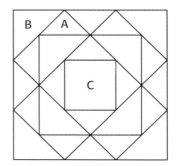

A ⊠ 4¼"   B ◺ 3⅞"   C ☐ 3½"

MARCH
4

Teacup
5" x 3½"

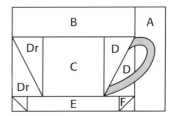

A ▭ 1½" × 4" C ▭ 2½" Dr ◹ PT-2 reversed F ◪ 1⅜"

B ▭ 1½" × 4½" D ◣ PT-2 E ▭ 1" × 3½"

Beacon Lights
12"

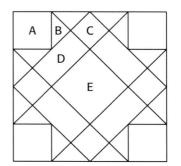

A ☐ 3½"   B ☒ 4¼"   C ☐ 2⅝"   D ☐ 2⅝" × 4¾"   E ☐ 4¾"

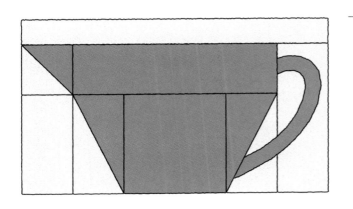

Creamer
6" x 3½"

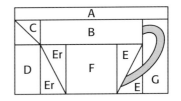

A ▭ 1" × 6½"   C ◨ 1⅞"   E ◺ PT-2   F ▭ 2½"

B ▭ 1½" × 4½"   D ▭ 1½" × 2½"   Er ◿ PT-2 reversed   G ▭ 1½" × 3½"

OCTOBER
27

Art Square
8"

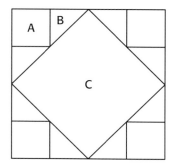

A ☐ 2½" B ◪ 2⅞" C ☐ 6³⁄₁₆"

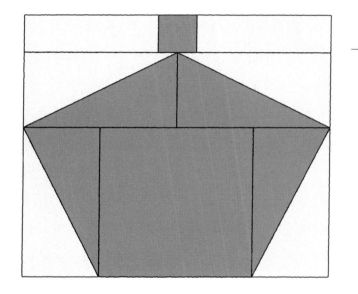

Sugar Bowl
4" x 3½"

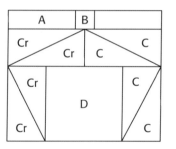

A ⬜ 1" × 2¼"   B ⬜ 1"   C ◺ PT-2   Cr ◿ PT-2 reversed   D ⬜ 2½"

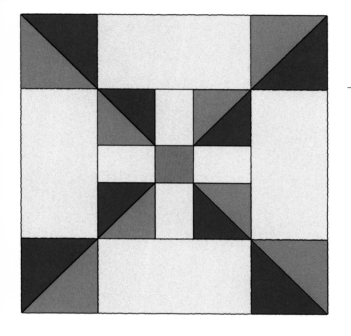

Whirling Square
8"

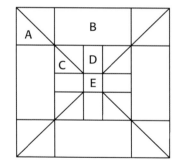

A ◨ 2⅞"   B ▭ 2½" × 4½"   C ◨ 2⅜"   D ▭ 1½" × 2"   E □ 1½"

Cut Glass Dish
12"

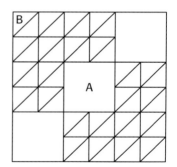

A □ 4½"   B ◺ 2⅞"

Light and Shadows
8"

A	B	

A ☐ 2½"   B ☐ 2½" × 4½"

MARCH
8

Cake Stand
8"

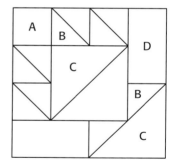

A ☐ 2½"   B ◹ 2⅞"   C ◹ 4⅞"   D ☐ 2½" × 4½"

OCTOBER
24

Missouri Star
8"

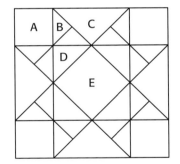

A ☐ 2½"   B ☒ 3¼"   C ☒ 5¼"   D ◩ 2⅞"   E ☐ 3⁵⁄₁₆"

Coffee Cup
6" x 4"

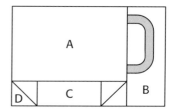

A ⬚ 3½" × 5"   B ⬚ 2" × 4½"   C ⬚ 1½" × 3"   D ◩ 1⅞"

OCTOBER
23

Star and Pinwheel
12"

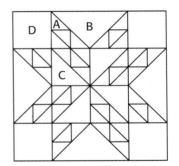

A ◹ 2⅜"   B ⊠ 7¼"   C ◹ 3⅞"   D ☐ 3½"

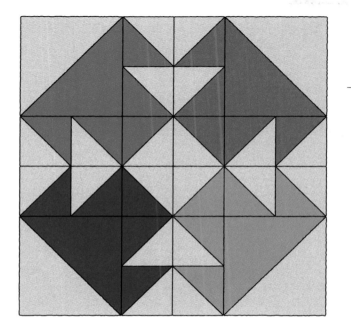

MARCH
10

Tea for Four
12"

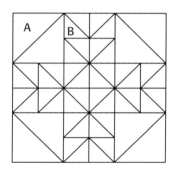

A ◿ 4⅞"   B ◿ 2⅞"

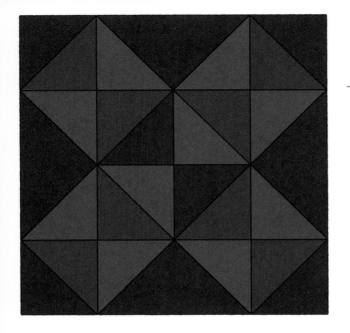

OCTOBER
22

Wheel of Time
10"

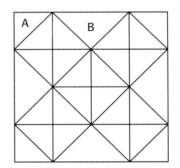

A ⬜ 3⅜"   B ⊠ 6¼"

MARCH
11

Northwind
9"

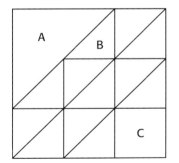

A ◩ 6⅞"   B ◩ 3⅞"   C ☐ 3½"

OCTOBER
21

Hither and Yon
12"

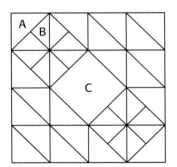

A ◩ 3⅞"   B ⊠ 4¼"   C ☐ 4¾"

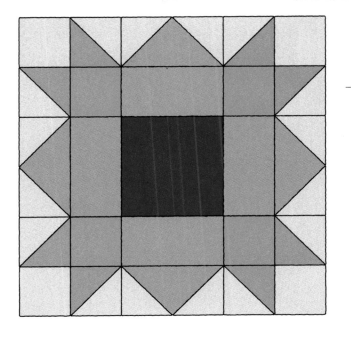

MARCH
12

Weathervane
12"

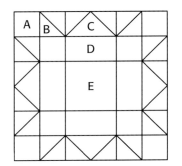

A ☐ 2½" B ◨ 2⅞" C ⊠ 5¼" D ▭ 2½" × 4½" E ☐ 4½"

OCTOBER
20

Dewey Dream Quilt
10"

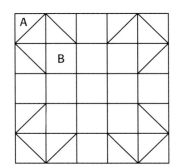

A ◹ 2⅞"   B ☐ 2½"

MARCH
13

Windmill
10"

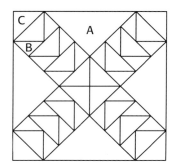

A ⊠ 7¼"   B ⊠ 3¼"   C ◩ 2⅞"

OCTOBER
19

Mineral Wells
12"

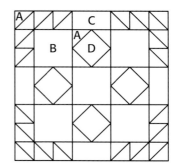

A ◩ 2³⁄₈"   B ☐ 3¹⁄₂"   C ▭ 2" × 3¹⁄₂"   D ☐ 2⁵⁄₈"

MARCH
14

Windmill Square
8"

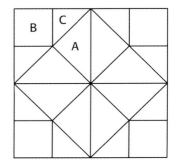

A ⊠ 5¼"   B ☐ 2½"   C ◹ 2⅞"

OCTOBER
18

Jefferson City
9"

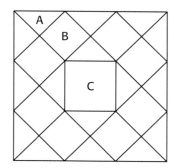

A ◻ 4¼"   B ◻ 2⅝"   C ◻ 3½"

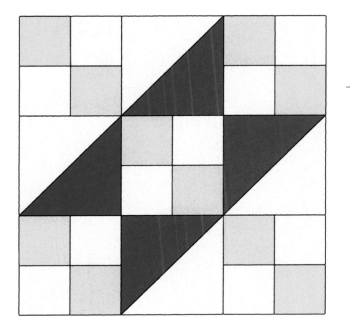

MARCH
15

Tail of Benjamin's Kite
9"

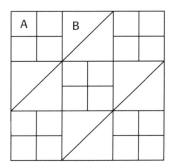

A ☐ 2"   B ◲ 3⅞"

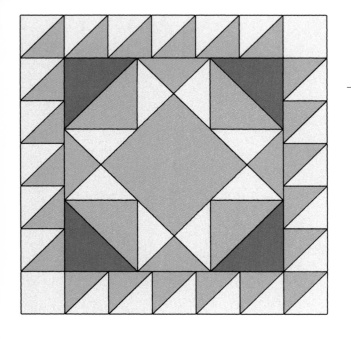

OCTOBER
17

Queen Victoria's Crown
13⅛"

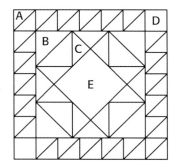

A ◿ 2¾" B ◿ 4" C ⧄ 4⅜" D ☐ 2⅜" E ☐ 4¹⁵⁄₁₆"

MARCH
16

Single Irish Chain
10"

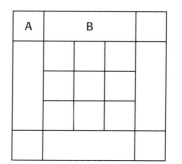

A ☐ 2½"   B ☐ 2½" × 6½"

OCTOBER
16

Anvil
9"

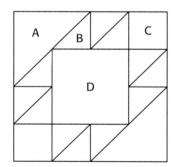

A $\boxed{\diagup}$ 5⅜"   B $\boxed{\diagup}$ 3⅛"   C $\boxed{}$ 2¾"   D $\boxed{}$ 5"

MARCH
17

Shamrock
9"

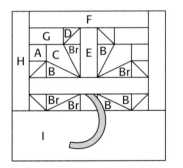

A ☐ 1½"

B ◣ PT-2

Br ◺ PT-2 reversed

C ⬠ PT-3

D ◨ 1⅞"

E ☐ 1½" × 3½"

F ☐ 1½" × 7½"

G ☐ 1½" × 2½"

H ☐ 1½" × 6½"

I ☐ 3½" × 9½"

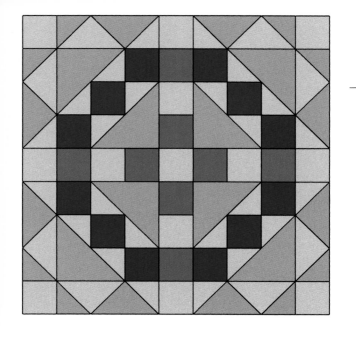

OCTOBER
15

Meeting House Square
9"

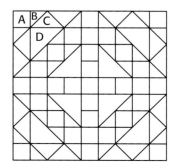

A ☐ 1½"   B ◺ 1⅞"   C ⊠ 3¼"   D ◺ 2⅞"

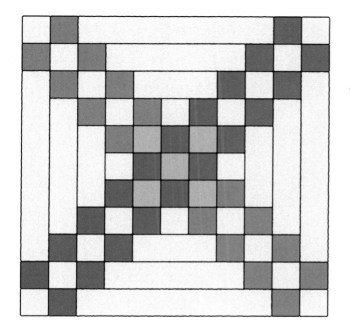

MARCH
18

Double Irish Chain
11"

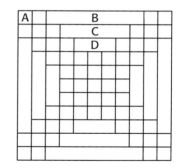

A ☐ 1½"   B ☐ 1½" × 7½"   C ☐ 1½" × 5½"   D ☐ 1½" × 3½"

OCTOBER
14

Table for Four
11"

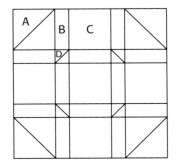

A ◪ 3⅞"   B ▭ 1½" × 3½"   C ☐ 3½"   D ◪ 1⅞"

MARCH
19

**Aunt Mary's
Double Irish Chain**
12"

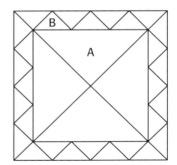

A ◻ 10¼"   B ◻ 4¼"

OCTOBER
13

Spider's Den
12"

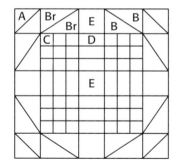

A ☐ 2⅞"   Br ◿ PT-5 reversed   D ▭ 1½" × 2½"
B ◺ PT-5   C ☐ 1½"   E ☐ 2½"

Bird of Paradise
12"

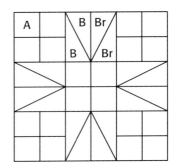

A ☐ 2½"   B ◸ PT-1   Br ◹ PT-1 reversed

OCTOBER
12

Spider
9"

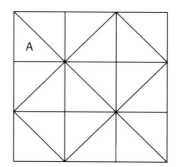

A ◻ 3⅞"

MARCH
21

Dutchman's Puzzle
10"

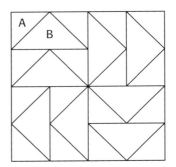

A ◻ 3⅜"   B ⊠ 6¼"

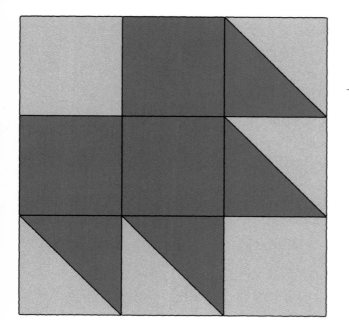

OCTOBER
11

Tea Leaf
9"

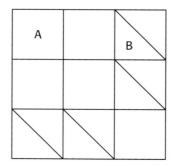

A □ 3½"   B ◺ 3⅞"

MARCH
22

Spring Has Come
12"

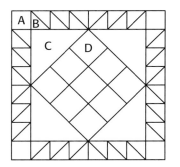

A ☐ 2"   B ◪ 2⅜"   C ◪ 5⅜"   D ☐ 2⅝"

OCTOBER
10

Medieval Walls
9"

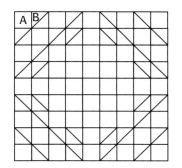

A ☐ 1½"   B ◺ 1⅞"

Road to Oklahoma
8"

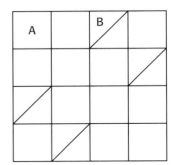

A ☐ 2½"   B ◪ 2⅞"

OCTOBER
9

Mrs. Keller's Nine Patch
10"

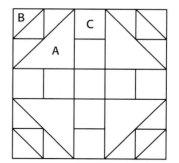

A � 4⅞"   B � 2⅞"   C ☐ 2½"

Rocky Road
9"

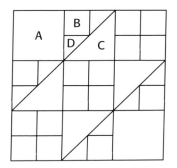

A ☐ 3½"   B ☐ 2"   C ◻ 3⅞"   D ◻ 2⅜"

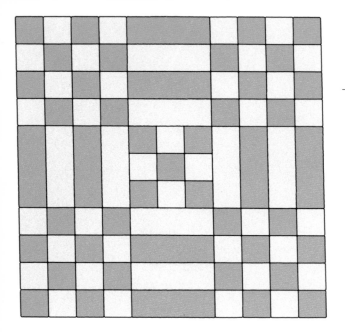

OCTOBER
8

Golden Gate
11"

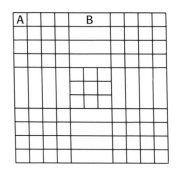

A ☐ 1½"   B ☐ 1½" × 3½"

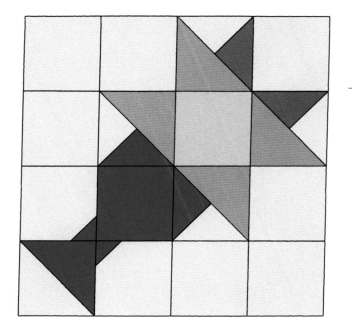

MARCH
25

Vase of Flowers
12"

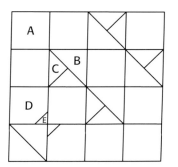

A ☐ 3½" B ◩ 3⅞" C ⊠ 4¼" D ☐ 3½" / TT-3 E ◩ 1⅞"

OCTOBER
7

Ozark Trail
10"

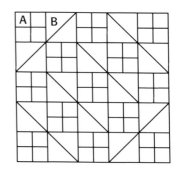

A ☐ 1½"   B ◺ 2⅞"

Beggar's Blocks
9"

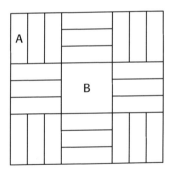

A [ ] 1½" × 3½"   B [ ] 3½"

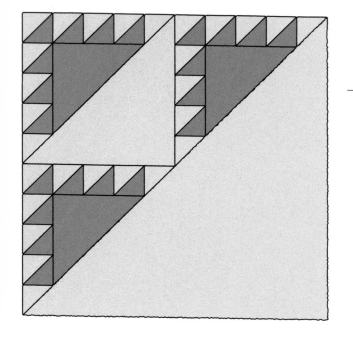

OCTOBER
6

Maryland Beauty
10"

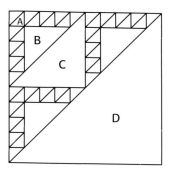

A ◪ 1⅞"   B ◪ 3⅞"   C ◪ 5⅞"   D ◪ 10⅞"

Bird's Nest
10"

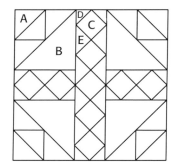

A ◹ 2⅞"   B ◹ 4⅞"   C ☐ 1¹⁵⁄₁₆"   D ◹ 1⅞"   E ◨ 3¼"

OCTOBER
5

Triangle Weave
8"

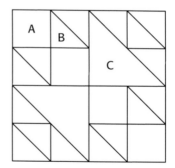

A ☐ 2½"   B ◿ 2⅞"   C ◿ 4⅞"

MARCH
28

Jacob's Ladder
8"

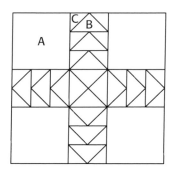

A ☐ 3½"   B ⊠ 3¼"   C ◿ 1⅞"

OCTOBER
4

Chisholm Trail
8"

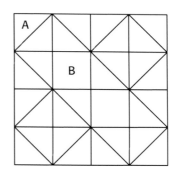

A ◺ 2⅞"   B ☐ 2½"

MARCH
29

Square and Star
12"

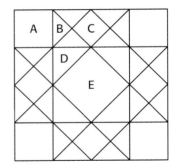

A ☐ 3½" B ☒ 4¼" C ☐ 2⅝" D ◩ 3⅞" E ☐ 4¾"

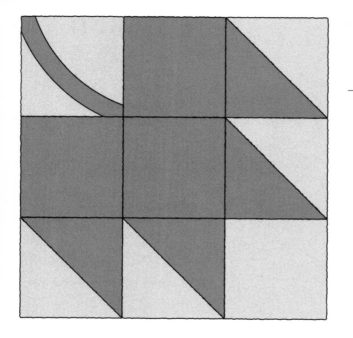

OCTOBER

3

Autumn Leaf
9"

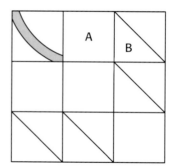

A ☐ 3½"   B ◹ 3⅞"

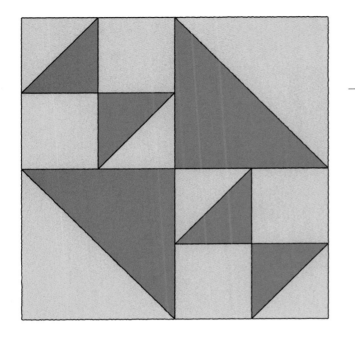

Crosses and Losses
8"

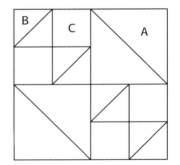

A ◩ 4⅞"   B ◩ 2⅞"   C ☐ 2½"

OCTOBER

2

Maple Leaf
9"

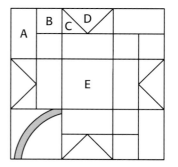

A ▭ 2" × 3½"   B ▢ 2"   C ◩ 2⅜"   D ⊠ 4¼"   E ▢ 3½"

MARCH
31

Snail's Trail
12"

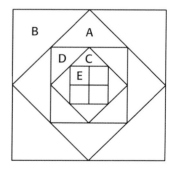

A ⊠ 7¼"   B ◩ 6⅞"   C ⊠ 4¼"   D ◩ 3⅞"   E ☐ 2"

OCTOBER
1

Autumn Tints
10½"

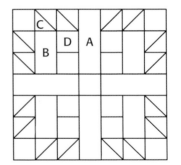

A ⬜ 2" × 5"   B ⬜ 2" × 3½"   C ◿ 2⅜"   D ⬜ 2"

Spring
April-June

Pretty pastel quilts become an instant favorite when springtime arrives. Along with Easter-themed blocks, April includes a variety of well-known and loved traditional designs. May blocks are filled with delightful flower and garden arrangements (complete with a birdhouse and watering can). For Mother's Day, create blocks that honor the special women in your life. You'll also find blocks to commemorate Memorial Day. June is the month for summer brides, so we've included blocks based on timeless, romantic themes. Other designs celebrate Father's Day, graduations, and the beginning of summer.

Autumn
October-December

With temperatures cooling off and daylight dwindling, October blocks pay homage to many autumn favorites, including the beautiful falling leaves that mark the change in season. And what would October be without a special selection of block "treats" for Halloween? Designs that celebrate Thanksgiving are included, along with a collection of blocks featuring harvest themes and Veterans Day tributes. And finally, to celebrate the much-anticipated Christmas holiday, December's blocks are brimming with visions of pine trees, whimsical angels, jolly Santas, and dancing stars you'll want to make a wish on.

APRIL
1

Fool's Puzzle
9"

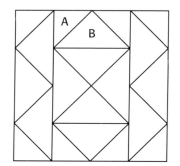

A ◻ 3⅛"   B ⊠ 5¾"

SEPTEMBER
30

Texas Puzzle
9"

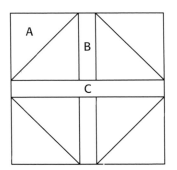

A ◻ 4⅞"   B ▭ 1½" × 4½"   C ▭ 1½" × 9½"

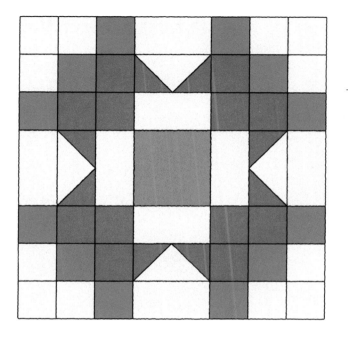

APRIL

2

April Tulips
16"

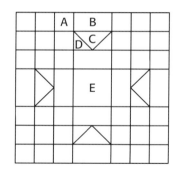

A ☐ 2½" B ☐ 2½" × 4½" C ⊠ 5¼" D ◩ 2⅞" E ☐ 4½"

SEPTEMBER
29

Premium Star
10"

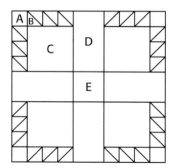

A ☐ 1½"   B ◲ 1⅞"   C ☐ 3½"   D ▭ 2½" × 4½"   E ☐ 2½"

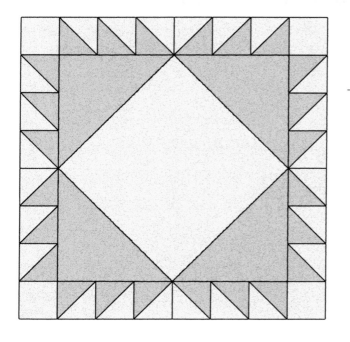

APRIL
3

Sunshine
16"

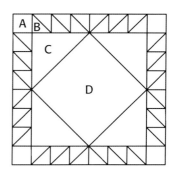

A ☐ 2½"   B ◩ 2⅞"   C ◩ 6⅞"   D ☐ 9"

SEPTEMBER
28

Queen's Crown
10"

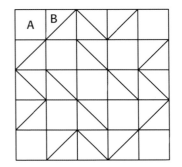

A ☐ 2½"   B ◺ 2⅞"

APRIL
4

Hill and Crag
10"

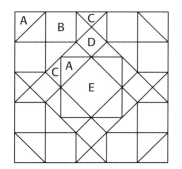

A ◰ 2⅞" B ☐ 2½" C ⊠ 3¼" D ☐ 1¹⁵⁄₁₆" E ☐ 3⁵⁄₁₆"

Squash Blossom
12"

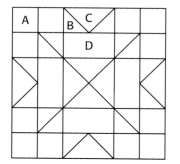

A ☐ 2½" B ◻ 2⅞" C ⊠ 5¼" D ▭ 2½" × 4½"

APRIL
5

Around the Corner
12"

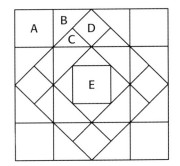

A ☐ 3½"   B ◪ 3⅞"   C ⊠ 4¼"   D ☐ 2⅝"   E ☐ 3½"

Wild Duck
8"

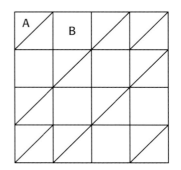

A ◸ 2⅞"   B ☐ 2½"

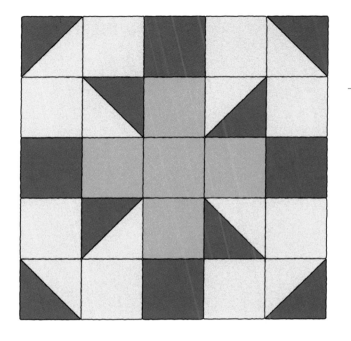

APRIL
6

Baton Rouge Square
10"

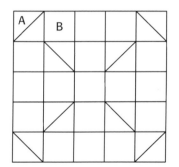

A ▱ 2⅞" B ☐ 2½"

SEPTEMBER
25

Hovering Hawks
8"

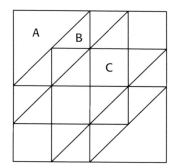

A ◹ 4⅞"   B ◹ 2⅞"   C ☐ 2½"

Salt Lake City
12"

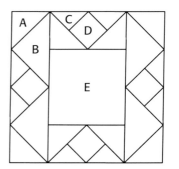

A ◻ 3⅞"   B ⊠ 7¼"   C ⊠ 4¼"   D ◻ 2⅝"   E ◻ 6½"

SEPTEMBER
24

Brown Goose
10"

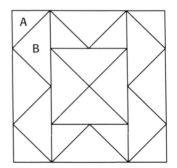

A ◺ 3⅜"   B ⊠ 6¼"

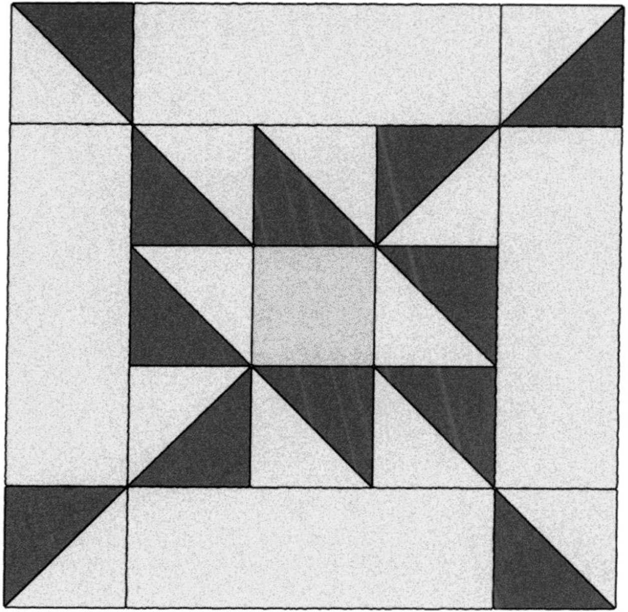

APRIL
8

Twister
10"

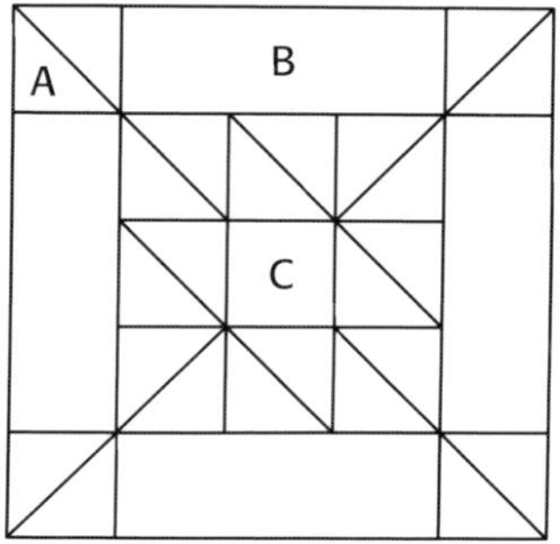

A 2⅞" B 2½" × 6½" C 2½"

SEPTEMBER
23

Winged Square
12"

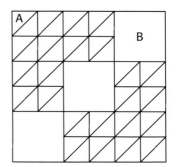

A ◹ 2⅞"   B ☐ 4½"

APRIL
9

Vermont
12"

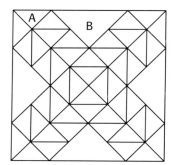

A ⊠ 4¼"   B ⊠ 7¼"

SEPTEMBER
22

Flock of Geese
10"

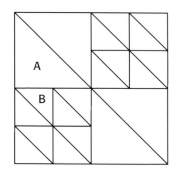

A ◻ 5⅞"   B ◻ 3⅜"

APRIL
10

Missouri Puzzle
13½"

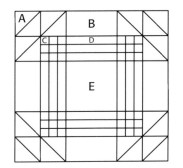

A ◩ 3⅛" B ▭ 2¾" × 5" C ☐ 1¼" D ▭ 1¼" × 5" E ☐ 5"

SEPTEMBER
21

Wild Goose Chase
10"

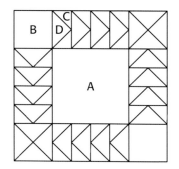

A ☐ 5½"   B ☐ 3"   C ◩ 2⅛"   D ⊠ 3¾"

Milky Way
12½"

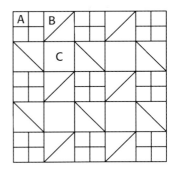

A ☐ 1¾"   B ◿ 3⅜"   C ☐ 3"

SEPTEMBER
20

Flying Geese
10"

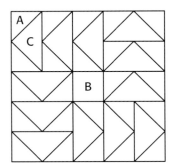

A ◸ 2⅞" B ☐ 2½" C ⊠ 5¼"

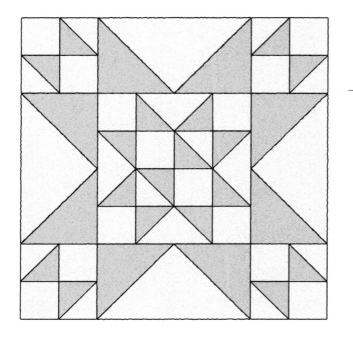

APRIL
12

Coronation
12"

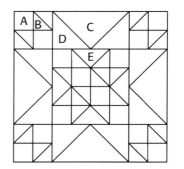

A ☐ 2" B ◺ 2⅜" C ⊠ 7¼" D ◺ 3⅞" E ⊠ 4¼"

SEPTEMBER
19

Birds in the Air
9"

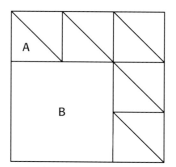

A ◸ 3⅞"   B ☐ 6½"

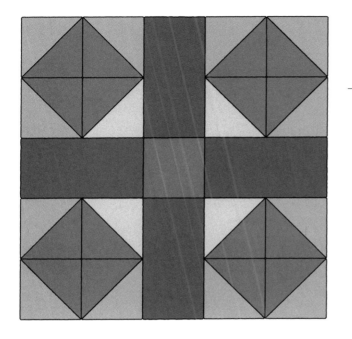

APRIL
13

Garden of Eden
10"

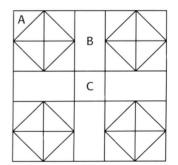

A ◩ 2⅞"   B ▭ 2½" × 4½"   C ▢ 2½"

SEPTEMBER
18

Geese in Flight
12"

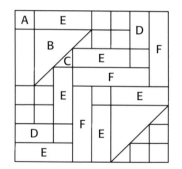

A ☐ 2" C ◩ 2⅜" E ▭ 2" × 5"

B ◩ 5⅜" D ▭ 2" × 3½" F ▭ 2" × 6½"

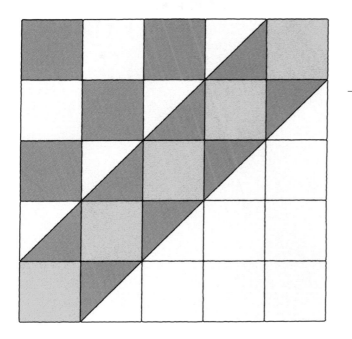

APRIL
14

King's Crown
10"

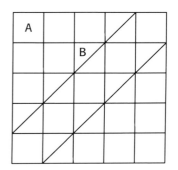

A ☐ 2½" B ◺ 2⅞"

SEPTEMBER
17

Johnny Round the Corner
9"

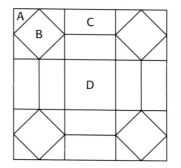

A ◹ 2³⁄₈"   B ☐ 2⁵⁄₈"   C ▭ 2" × 3¹⁄₂"   D ☐ 3¹⁄₂"

APRIL
15

Joseph's Coat
10"

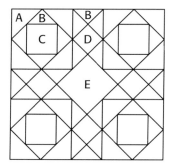

A ◿ 2⅞" B ⊠ 3¼" C ☐ 2½" D ☐ 1⅞" E ☐ 3⁵⁄₁₆"

SEPTEMBER
16

Thunder and Lightning
12"

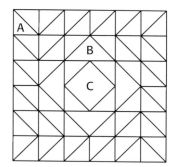

A ◻ 2⅞"   B ⊠ 5¼"   C ☐ 3⁵⁄₁₆"

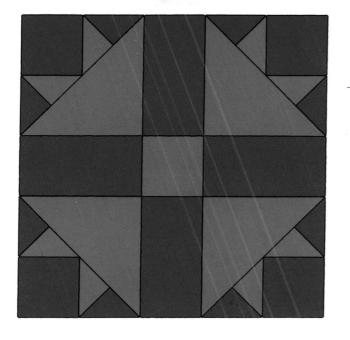

Cross and Crown
10"

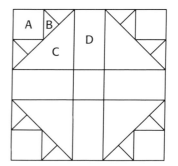

A ☐ 2½"   B ⊠ 3¼"   C ⊘ 4⅞"   D ☐ 2½" × 4½"

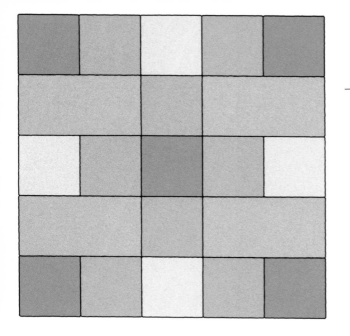

SEPTEMBER
15

Plaid
10"

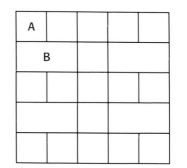

A ☐ 2½"   B ▭ 2½" × 4½"

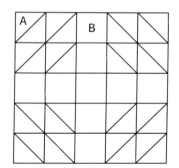

APRIL
17

Crown of Thorns
10"

A ◹ 2⅞"   B ☐ 2½"

SEPTEMBER
14

Hour Glass
9"

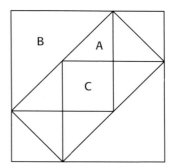

A ◩ 3⅞"   B ◩ 6⅞"   C ☐ 3½"

APRIL
18

Crossroads to Jericho
8"

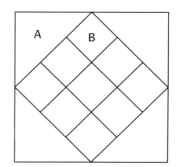

A ▱ 4⅞"   B ☐ 2⅜"

SEPTEMBER
13

Towers of Camelot
9"

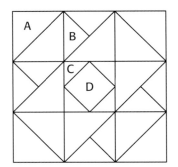

A ◹ 3⅞"   B ⊠ 4¼"   C ◹ 2⅜"   D ☐ 2⅝"

Alpine Cross
10"

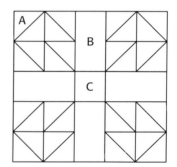

A B C labels within diagram

A ◻ 2⅞"   B ▭ 2½" × 4½"   C ☐ 2½"

SEPTEMBER
12

Queen's Petticoat
9"

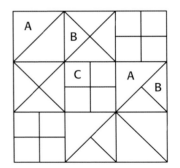

A ◻ 3⅞"   B ⊠ 4¼"   C ☐ 2"

APRIL
20

Devil's Claws
12"

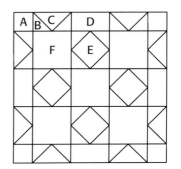

A ☐ 2"   B ◿ 2³⁄₈"   C ⊠ 4¹⁄₄"   D ▭ 2" × 3¹⁄₂"   E ☐ 2⁵⁄₈"   F ☐ 3¹⁄₂"

SEPTEMBER
11

Schoolhouse
12"

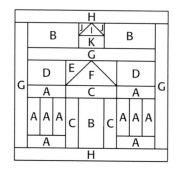

A ⬜ 1½" × 3½"
B ⬜ 2½" × 4½"
C ⬜ 1½" × 4½"

D ⬜ 2½" × 3½"
E ◨ 2⅞"
F ⊠ 5¼"

G ⬜ 1½" × 10½"
H ⬜ 1½" × 12½"
I ⊠ 3¼"

J ◨ 1⅞"
K ⬜ 1½" × 2½"

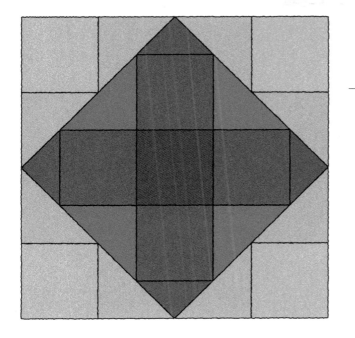

APRIL
21

Cross Within a Cross
12"

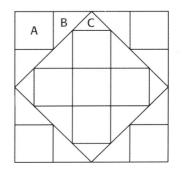

A □ 3½"   B ▱ 3⅞"   C ⊠ 4¼"

SEPTEMBER
10

E
7½"

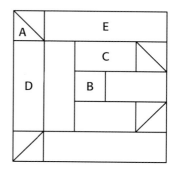

A ▱ 2⅜" B ▢ 2" C ▭ 2" × 3½" D ▭ 2" × 5" E ▭ 2" × 6½"

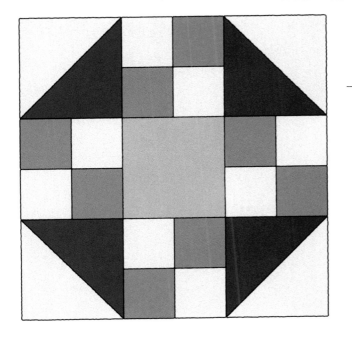

APRIL
22

Prairie Queen
9"

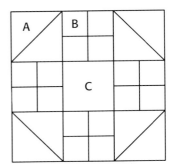

A ◻ 3⅞"   B ☐ 2"   C ☐ 3½"

SEPTEMBER
9

D
7½"

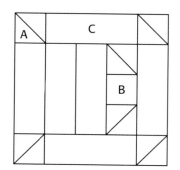

A ◿ 2⅜"   B ☐ 2"   C ▭ 2" × 5"

Corner Star
12¾"

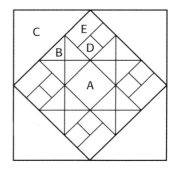

A ☐ 3½"   B ☒ 4¼"   C ◩ 7¼"   D ☐ 2"   E ▭ 2" × 3½"

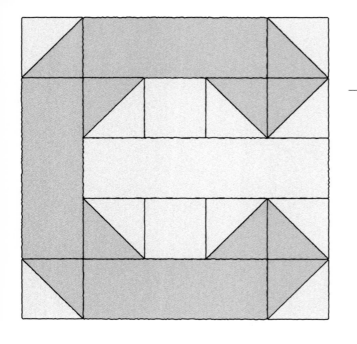

C
7½"

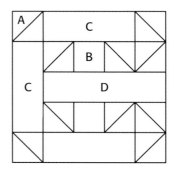

A ◿ 2⅜" B ☐ 2" C ▭ 2" × 5" D ▭ 2" × 6½"

APRIL
24

Delectable Mountains
10"

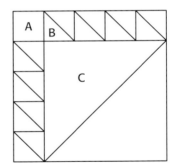

A ☐ 2½"   B ◹ 2⅞"   C ◹ 8⅞"

SEPTEMBER

7

B
7½"

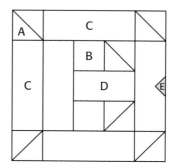

A ▱ 2⅜"   B ☐ 2"   C ▭ 2" × 5"   D ▭ 2" × 3½"   E ◁ AT-7

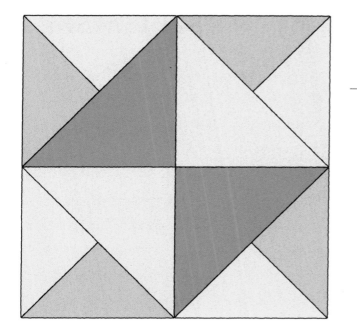

APRIL
25

Southern Belle
10"

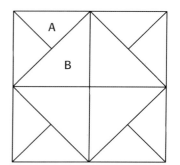

A ⊠ 6¼"   B ◺ 5⅞"

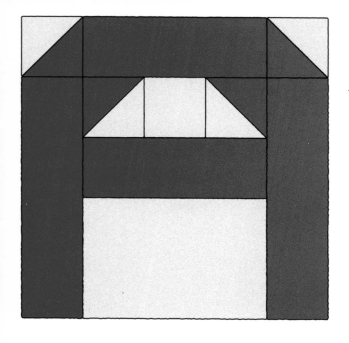

SEPTEMBER
6

A
7½"

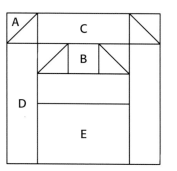

A ◹ 2⅜"   B ☐ 2"   C ▭ 2" × 5"   D ▭ 2" × 6½"   E ▭ 3½" × 5"

Swamp Angel
12"

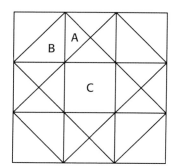

A ⊠ 5¼"   B ◿ 4⅞"   C ☐ 4½"

SEPTEMBER
5

School Boy
8" x 12"

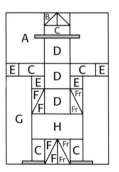

A	☐	3½" × 4½"	D	☐	2½"	Fr	◹	PT-2 reversed	Embroider face.
B	◺	1⅞"	E	☐	1½"	G	☐	2½" × 7½"	
C	☐	1½" × 2½"	F	◺	PT-2	H	☐	2½" × 4½"	

Arkansas Crossroads
8"

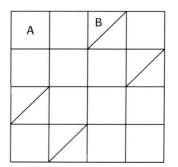

A ☐ 2½"   B ◹ 2⅞"

SEPTEMBER
4

School Girl
8" x 12"

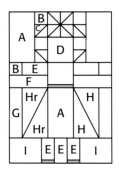

A [ ] 2½" × 4½"

B [ ] 1½"

C [◺] 1⅞"

D [ ] 2½"

E [ ] 1½" × 2½"

F [ ] 1½" × 3½"

G [ ] 1½" × 4½"

H [◹] PT-1

Hr [◸] PT-1 reversed

I [ ] 2½" × 3"

Embroider face;
add buttons and
lace on dress.

Northumberland Star
12"

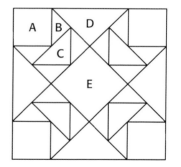

A ☐ 3½"   B ◻ 3"   C ⊠ 5½"   D ⊠ 7¼"   E ☐ 4¾"

SEPTEMBER
3

Old Home
11"

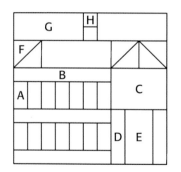

A ☐ 1½" × 2½" C ☐ 3½" × 4½" E ☐ 2½" × 4½" G ☐ 2½" × 5½"

B ☐ 1½" × 7½" D ☐ 1½" × 4½" F ◩ 2⅞" H ☐ 1½"

APRIL
29

Wyoming Valley Star
15"

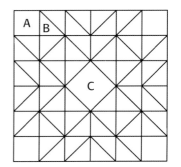

A ☐ 3"   B ◹ 3⅜"   C ☐ 4¹/₁₆"

SEPTEMBER
2

House on the Hill
12"

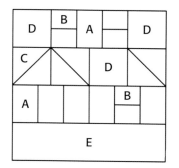

A ☐ 2½" × 3½"   B ☐ 2" × 2½"   C ◸ 3⅞"   D ☐ 3½"   E ☐ 3½" × 12½"

APRIL

30

Arizona
12"

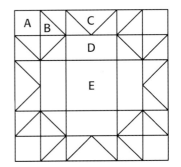

A ☐ 2½"   B ◲ 2⅞"   C ⊠ 5¼"   D ☐ 2½" × 4½"   E ☐ 4½"

SEPTEMBER
1

Little Red Schoolhouse
8"

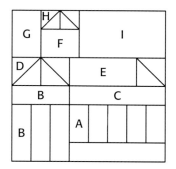

A ▢ 1½" × 2½"　　D ◪ 2⅜"　　G ▭ 2" × 3"

B ▢ 1½" × 3½"　　E ▭ 2" × 4"　　H ◪ 1⅞"

C ▭ 1½" × 5½"　　F ▢ 2" × 2½"　　I ▭ 3" × 5"

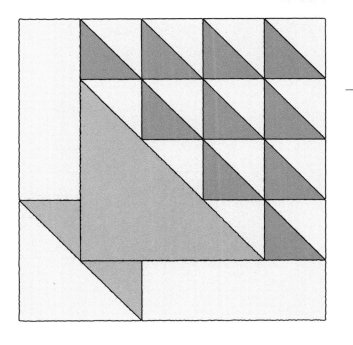

May Basket
5"

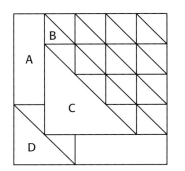

A ☐ 1½" × 3½"   B ◩ 1⅞"   C ◩ 3⅞"   D ◩ 2⅞"

31

Children's Delight
10"

	A	B	
D		C	

A ☐ 2½"   B ▭ 2½" × 4½"   C ☐ 4½"   D ▭ 2½" × 8½"

MAY

2

May Basket
6"

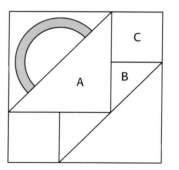

A ▢ 4⅞" B ▢ 2⅞" C ▢ 2½"

AUGUST
30

Hopscotch
8"

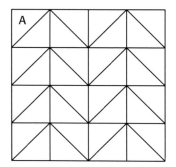

A ◿ 2⅞"

MAY
3

Flower Pot
10"

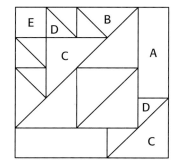

A ☐ 2½" × 6½" B ☒ 5¼" C ◹ 4⅞" D ◹ 2⅞" E ☐ 2½"

AUGUST
29

Spinning Tops
10"

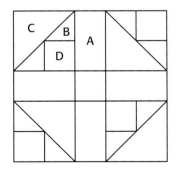

A ☐ 2½" × 4½"   B ◸ 2⅞"   C ◿ 4⅞"   D ☐ 2½"

MAY
4

Flower Basket
10"

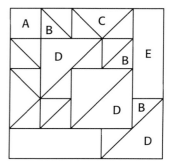

A ☐ 2½" B ◻ 2⅞" C ⊠ 5¼" D ◻ 4⅞" E ☐ 2½" × 6½"

AUGUST
28

School Girl's Puzzle
10"

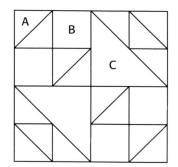

A ◪ 3⅜"   B ☐ 3"   C ◪ 5⅞"

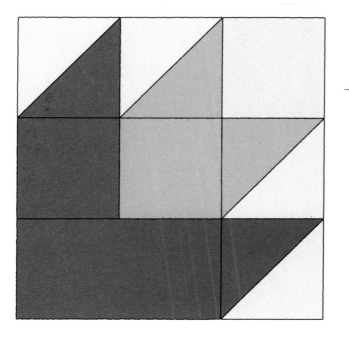

MAY
5

Flower Bud
6"

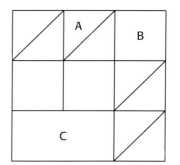

A ◩ 2⅞" B ☐ 2½" C ▭ 2½" × 4½"

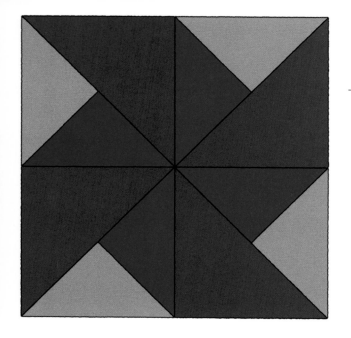

AUGUST
27

Whirligig
8"

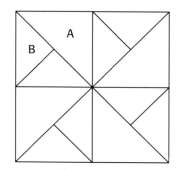

A ⬜ 4⅞"   B ⬛ 5¼"

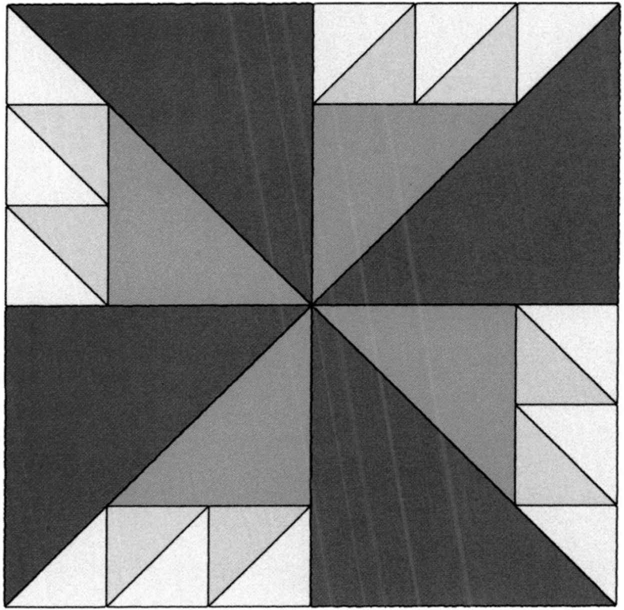

MAY
6

Rosebud
9"

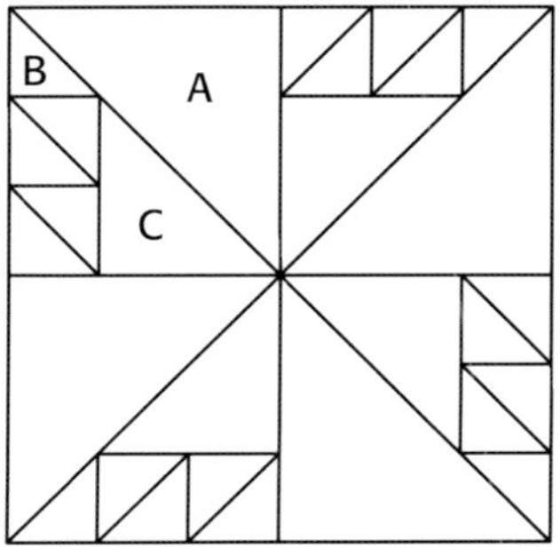

A ◫ 5⅜" B ◫ 2⅜" C ◫ 3⅞"

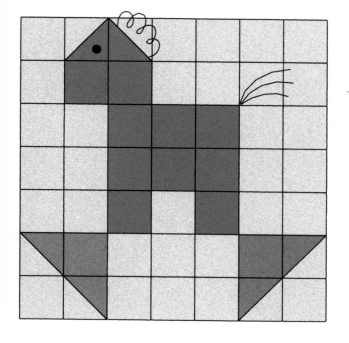

AUGUST
26

Rocking Horse
10½"

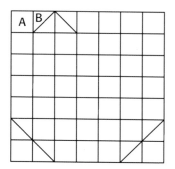

A ☐ 2"   B ◸ 2⅜"

Embroider tail and mane. Add small button for eye.

MAY

7

Pot of Flowers
10"

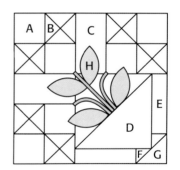

A ☐ 2½" C ▭ 2½" × 4½" E ▭ 1½" × 4½" G ◪ 2⅞"

B ⊠ 3¼" D ◪ 5⅞" F ◪ 1⅞" H ⬯ AT-3

AUGUST
25

Swing in the Center
9"

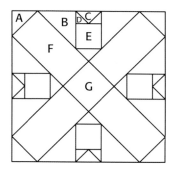

A ◹ 2⅜"   C ⊠ 2¾"   E ☐ 2"

B ◹ 3⅛"   D ◹ 1⅝"   F ☐ 2⅝" × 4¾"

G ☐ 2⅝"

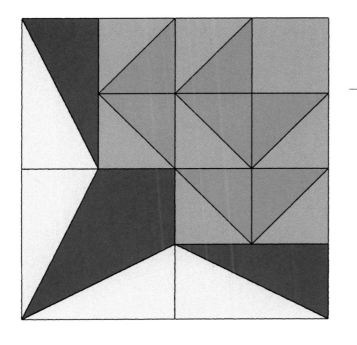

Nancy's Nosegay
8"

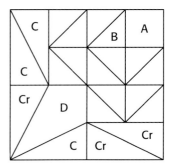

A ☐ 2½"　　B ◩ 2⅞"　　C ◺ PT-1　　Cr ◿ PT-1 reversed　　D ◁ PT-4

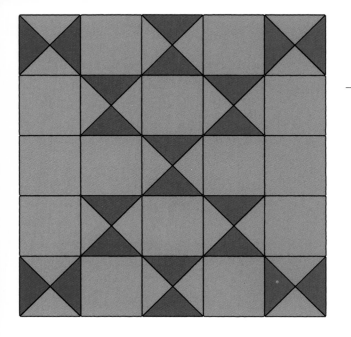

AUGUST
24

Clown
10"

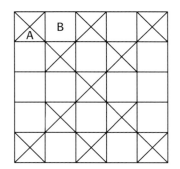

A ⊠ 3¼"   B ☐ 2½"

MAY
9

Daffodil
8"

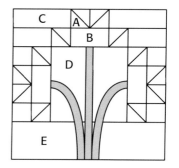

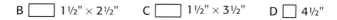

A ◿ 1⅞"   B ▭ 1½" × 2½"   C ▭ 1½" × 3½"   D ☐ 4½"   E ▭ 2½" × 8½"

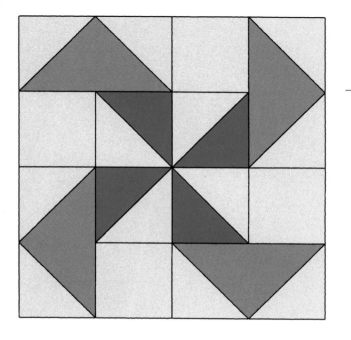

AUGUST
23

Seesaw
8"

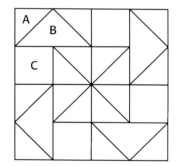

A ⬚ 2⅞"   B ⊠ 5¼"   C ☐ 2½"

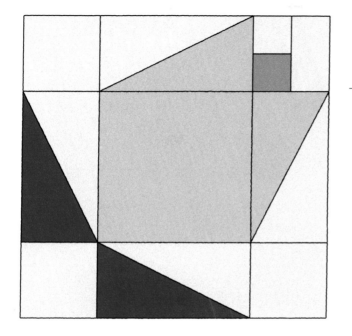

MAY
10

Magnolia Bud
8"

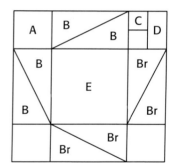

A ▢ 2½" Br ◺ PT-1 reversed D ▭ 1½" × 2½"
B ◹ PT-1 C ▢ 1½" E ▢ 4½"

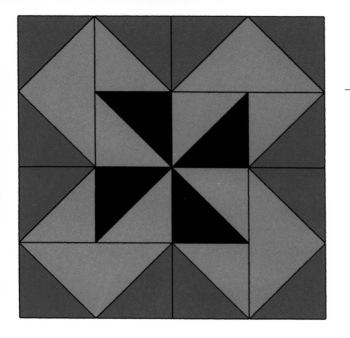

AUGUST
22

Jack in the Box
10"

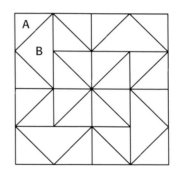

A ▱ 3⅜" B ⊠ 6¼"

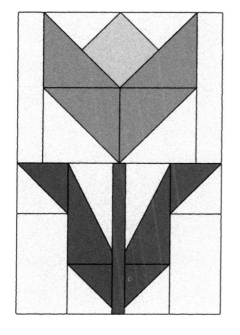

MAY
11

Tulip Time
8" x 12"

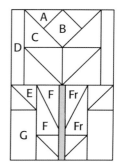

A ⊠ 4¼"   C ◰ 3⅞"   E ◰ 2⅞"   Fr ◸ PT-1 reversed

B ☐ 2⅝"   D ☐ 1½" × 6½"   F ◹ PT-1   G ☐ 2½" × 4½"

AUGUST
21

Cat's Cradle
12"

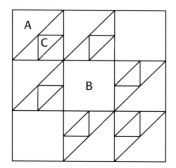

A ◻ 4⅞"   B ☐ 4½"   C ◻ 2⅞"

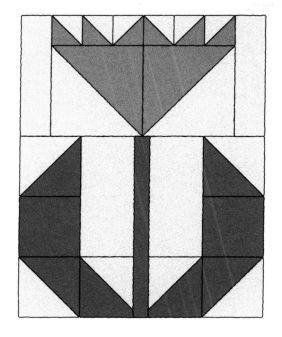

Tulip
8" x 10"

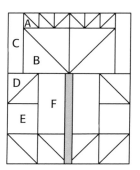

A ◻ 1⅞"   C ▭ 1½" × 4½"   E ◻ 2½"
B ◻ 3⅞"   D ◻ 2⅞"   F ◻ 4½"

Ferris Wheel
12"

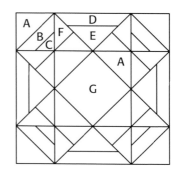

A ◹ 3⅞"

B ⬡ 1⁹⁄₁₆" × 5½" / TT-4

C ◹ 2⅜"

D ⬡ 1½" × 7³⁄₁₆" / TT-5

E ⊠ 5¼"

F ⊠ 4¼"

G ☐ 4¾"

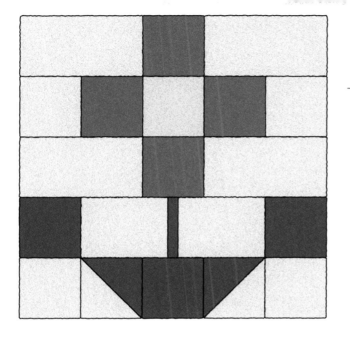

Flower Pot
5"

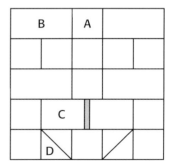

A ☐ 1½"   B ☐ 1½" × 2½"   C ☐ 1½" × 3½"   D ◪ 1⅞"

AUGUST
19

**Merry Go Round
8"**

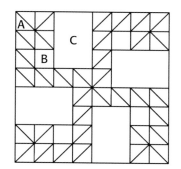

A ◰ 1⅞"   B ☐ 1½"   C ▭ 2½" × 3½"

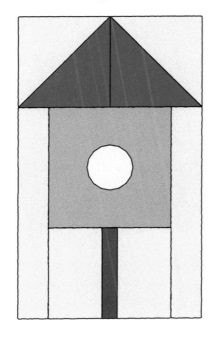

MAY
14

Bird House
6" x 10"

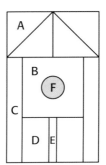

A ◻ 3⁷⁄₈"   C ▭ 1½" × 7½"   E ▭ 1" × 3½"
B ◻ 4½"   D ▭ 2¼" × 3½"   F ◯ 1½" diameter circle (appliqué)

AUGUST
18

Fireflies
8"

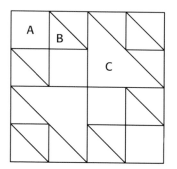

A ☐ 2½" B ◩ 2⅞" C ◩ 4⅞"

MAY
15

Watering Can
11"

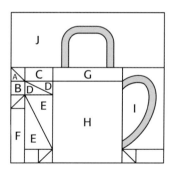

A ⬜ 1⅞"

B ⬜ 1½"

C ▭ 1½" × 2½"

D ◺ PT-2

E ◹ PT-1

F ▭ 1½" × 4½"

G ▭ 1½" × 5½"

H ▭ 5½" × 6½"

I ▭ 3½" × 6½"

J ▭ 4½" × 11½"

Building Blocks
10"

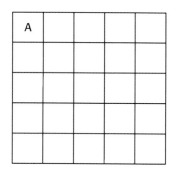

A ☐ 2½"

MAY
16

Aunt Sukey's Choice
12"

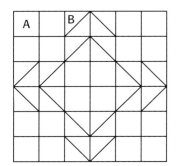

A ☐ 2½"   B ◩ 2⅞"

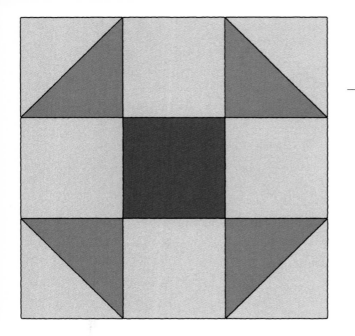

AUGUST
16

Shoo Fly
9"

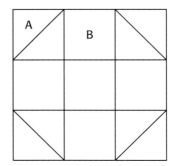

A ◻ 3⅞"   B ☐ 3½"

Sister's Choice
10"

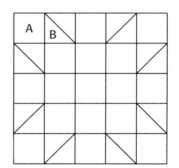

A □ 2½"   B ◩ 2⅞"

AUGUST
15

Path Through the Woods
10"

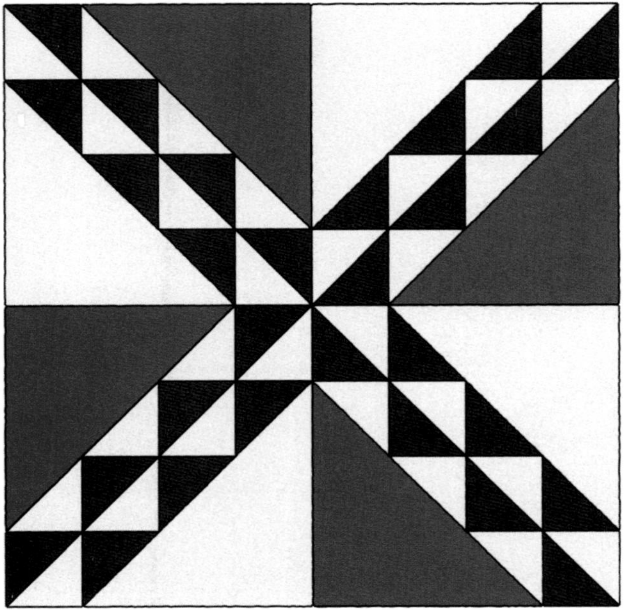

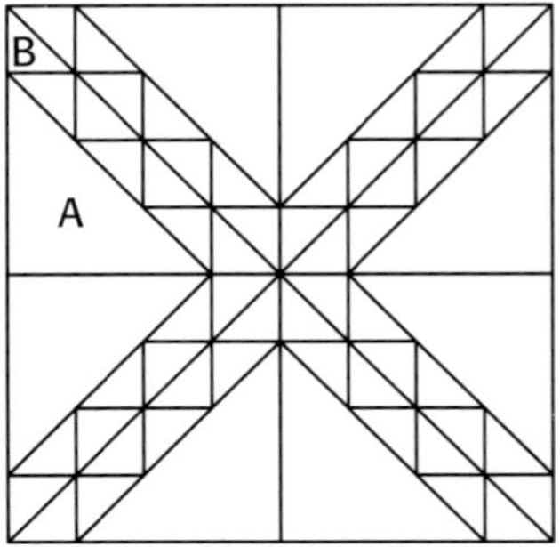

A 4⅝"   B 2⅛"

Grandmother's Choice
10"

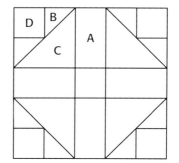

A ▢ 2½" × 4½"   B ◲ 2⅞"   C ◲ 4⅞"   D ▢ 2½"

AUGUST
14

Overall Bill
4"

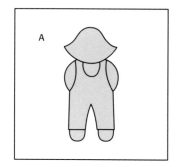

A ☐ 4½"

Appliqué templates on page 20.

MAY
19

Grandmother's Favorite
10"

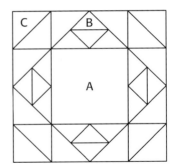

A ☐ 5½" B ☒ 3¾" C ◻ 3⅜"

AUGUST
13

Sunbonnet Sue
4"

A   ☐   4½"

Appliqué templates on page 20.

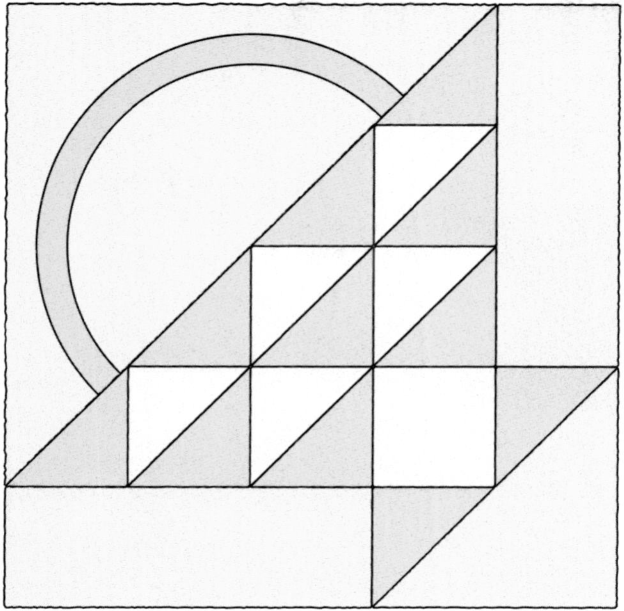

MAY 20

Grandmother's Basket
10"

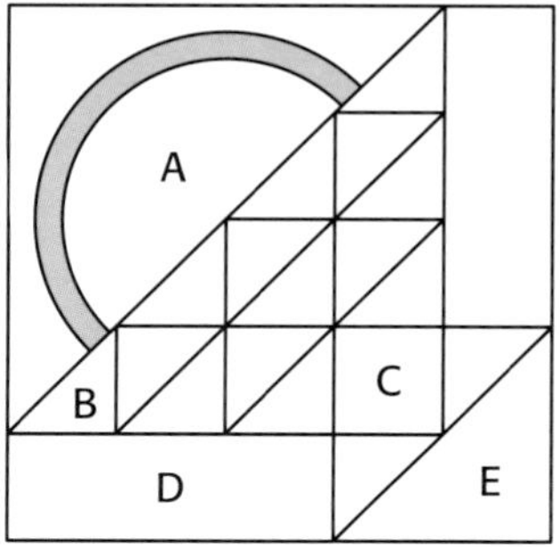

A ◸ 8⅞" B ◸ 2⅞" C □ 2½" D ▭ 2½" × 6½" E ◸ 4⅞"

AUGUST
12

Country Farm
9"

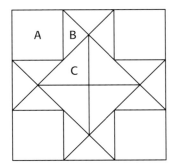

A ☐ 3½" B ☒ 4¼" C ☒ 5½"

Lady of the Lake
10"

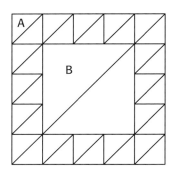

A ◹ 2⅞"   B ◹ 6⅞"

AUGUST
11

Our Village Green
10"

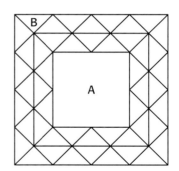

A ☐ 5½"   B ☒ 3¾"

Mother's Choice
12"

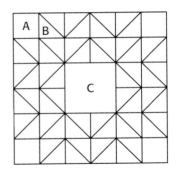

A ☐ 2½" B ◱ 2⅞" C ☐ 4½"

AUGUST
10

Market Square
16"

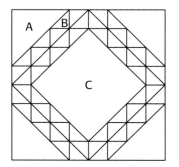

A ◹ 6⅞"   B ◹ 2⅞"   C ☐ 9"

Mother's Favorite
12"

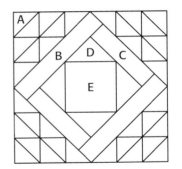

A ◹ 2⁷⁄₈" B ▭ 1¹⁵⁄₁₆" × 9" C ▭ 1¹⁵⁄₁₆" × 6¹⁄₈" D ⊠ 5¹⁄₄" E ☐ 4¹⁄₂"

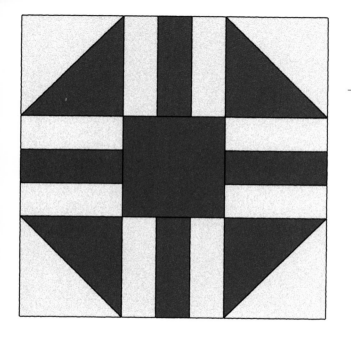

Paths and Stiles
9"

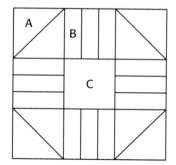

A ◻ 3⅞"   B ▭ 1½" × 3½"   C ◻ 3½"

MAY
24

Mother's Dream
18"

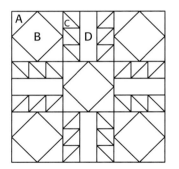

A ◣ 3⅞" B ☐ 4¾" C ◣ 2⅞" D ☐ 2½" × 6½"

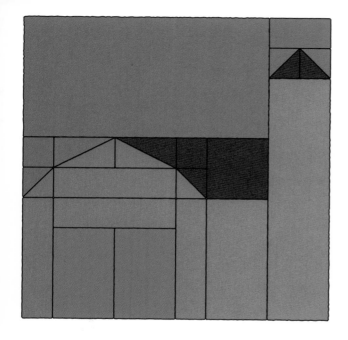

AUGUST
8

Country Barn
10"

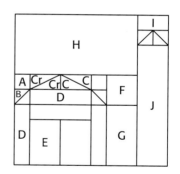

A ☐ 1½"

B ◨ 1⅞"

C ◺ PT-2

Cr ◿ PT-2 reversed

D ☐ 1½" × 4½"

E ☐ 2½" × 3½"

F ☐ 2½"

G ☐ 2½" × 4½"

H ☐ 4½" × 8½"

I ☐ 1½" × 2½"

J ☐ 2½" × 8½"

MAY
25

Mother's Fancy
14"

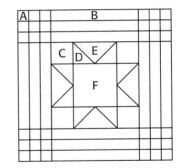

A ☐ 1½"

B ▭ 1½" × 8½"

C ☐ 2½"

D ◩ 2⅞"

E ⊠ 5¼"

F ☐ 4½"

AUGUST
7

Country Roads
10½"

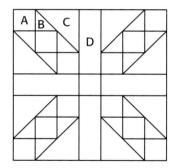

A ☐ 2"   B ◪ 2⅜"   C ◪ 3⅞"   D ▭ 2" × 5"

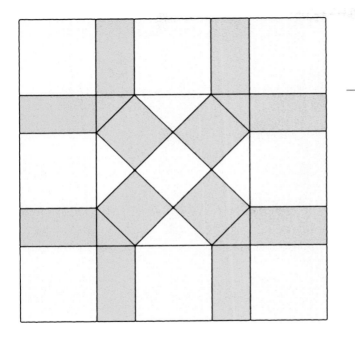

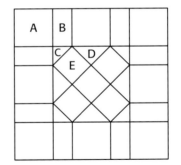

MAY
26

Mother's Own
8"

A ☐ 2½" B ▭ 1½" × 2½" C ◩ 1⅞" D ⊠ 3¼" E ☐ 1¹⁵⁄₁₆"

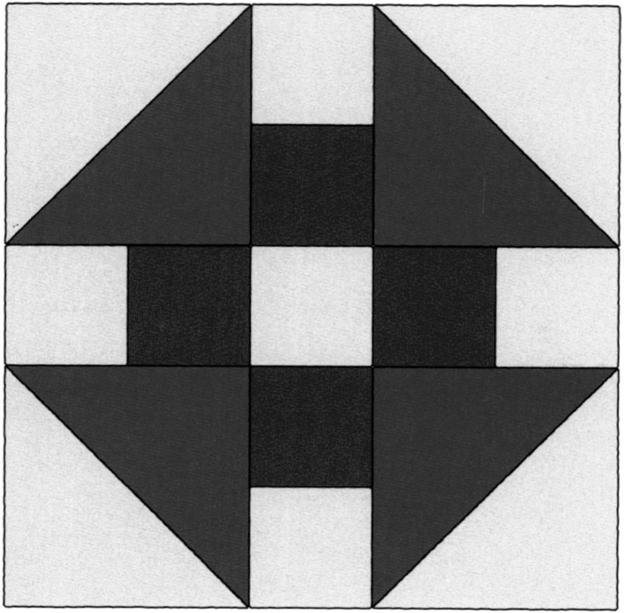

AUGUST
6

Churn Dash
7½"

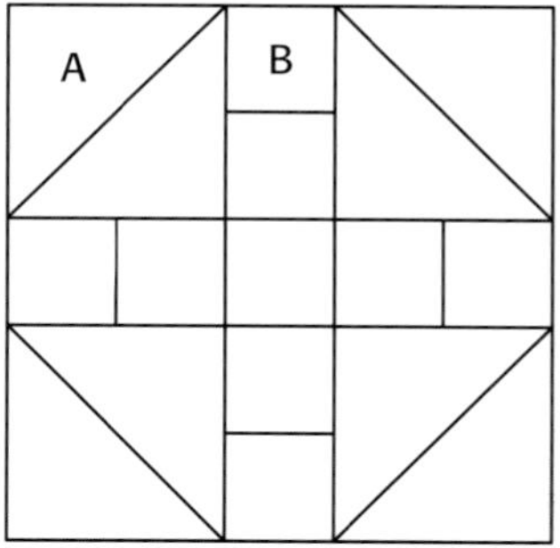

A ◿ 3⅞"   B □ 2"

MAY
27

Duck and Ducklings
12"

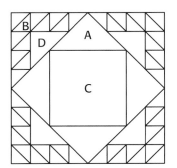

A ⊠ 7¼"   B ◺ 2⅜"   C ☐ 6½"   D ◺ 3⅞"

AUGUST
5

Waterwheel
7"

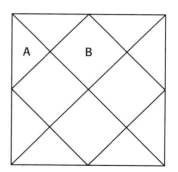

A ⊠ 4¾"   B ☐ 3"

Hen and Chicks
10"

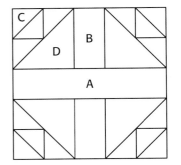

A ▢ 2½" × 10½"   B ▢ 2½" × 4½"   C ◫ 2⅞"   D ◫ 4⅞"

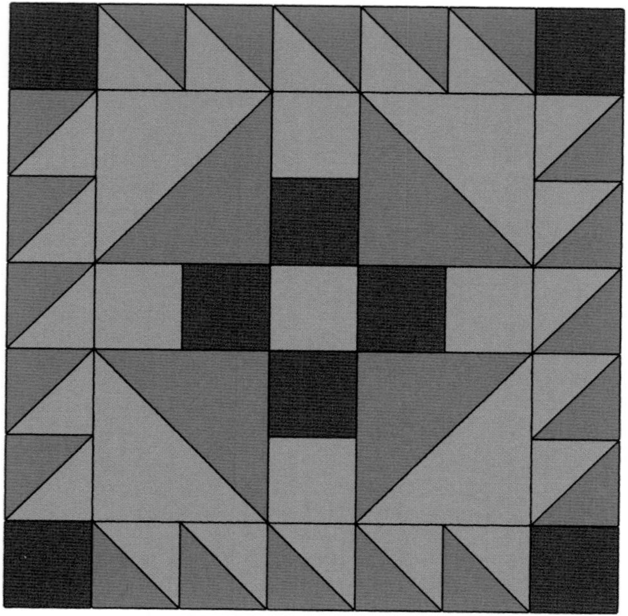

AUGUST 4

Prickly Pear
10½"

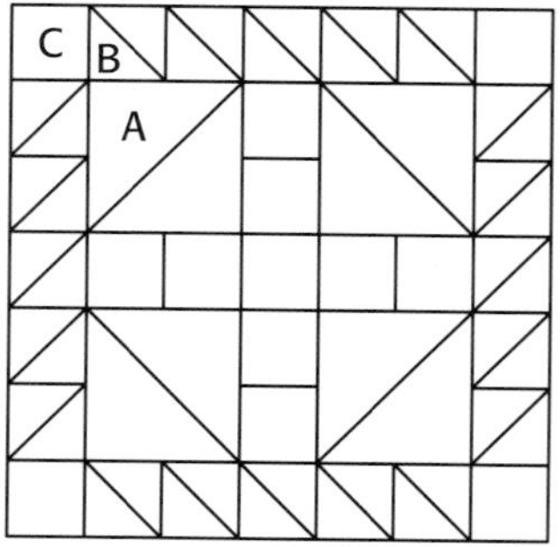

A ◪ 3⅞" B ◪ 2⅜" C ☐ 2"

Memory
12"

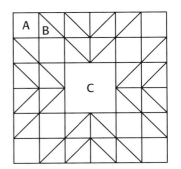

A ☐ 2½"   B ◺ 2⅞"   C ☐ 4½"

AUGUST
3

Grape Basket
10"

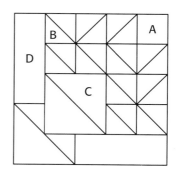

A ☐ 2½" B ◲ 2⅞" C ◲ 4⅞" D ▭ 2½" × 6½"

Memory Block
10"

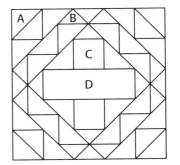

A ◿ 2⅞"   B ⊠ 3¼"   C ☐ 2½"   D ▭ 2½" × 6½"

AUGUST
2

Old-Fashioned Fruit Basket
12"

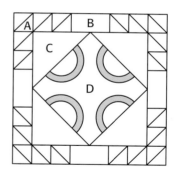

A ◫ 2⅜" B ▭ 2" × 3½" C ◫ 5⅜" D ▢ 6⅞"

Memory Wreath
12"

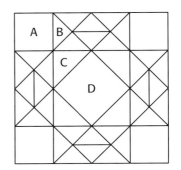

A ☐ 3½"   B ⊠ 4¼"   C ◹ 3⅞"   D ☐ 4¾"

AUGUST
1

Corn and Beans
12"

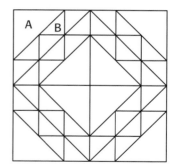

A ◿ 4⅞"   B ◿ 2⅞"

JUNE

1

Wedding Ring
10"

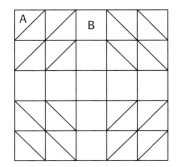

A ◿ 2⅞"   B ☐ 2½"

JULY
31

Lightning in the Hills
12"

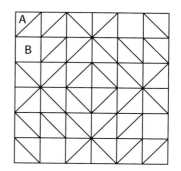

A ◹ 2⅞"   B ☐ 2½"

JUNE
2

Bridal Wreath
6"

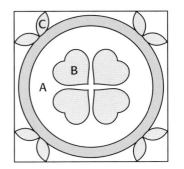

A ▢ 6½"   B ♡ AT-4   C ⬯ AT-5

Flying Fish
12"

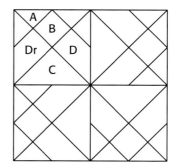

A ⊠ 4¼"   B ☐ 2⅝"   C ⊠ 7¼"   D ◻ PT-6   Dr ◺ PT-6 reversed

JUNE
3

Wedding March
18"

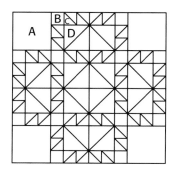

A ☐ 5"   B ☐ 2"   C ◪ 2⅜"   D ◪ 3⅞"

Flyfoot
8"

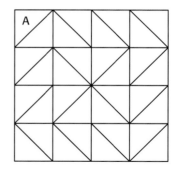

A ◻ 2⅞"

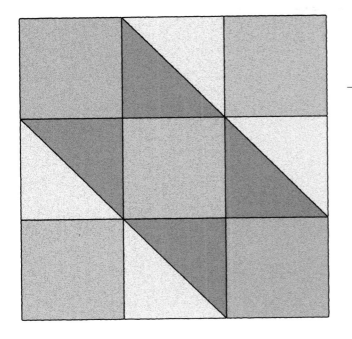

JUNE
4

Contrary Wife
9"

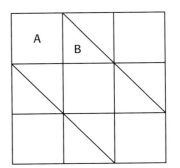

A ☐ 3½" B ◻ 3⅞"

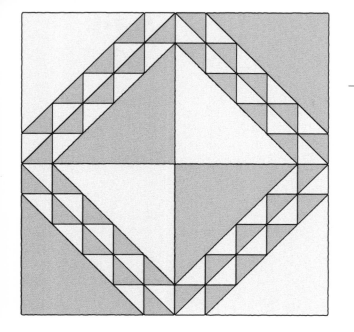

JULY
28

Sun and Shade
15"

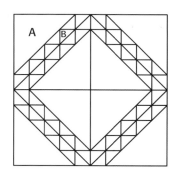

A ▱ 6⅞"   B ▱ 2⅜"

JUNE
5

Steps to the Altar
12"

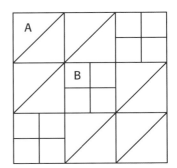

A ◸ 4⅞"   B ☐ 2½"

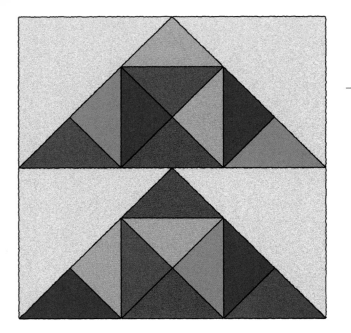

Hill and Valley
9"

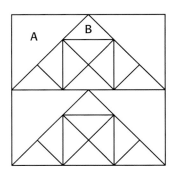

A ⬩ 5⅜"   B ⬩ 4¼"

JUNE
6

Bachelor's Puzzle
11¼"

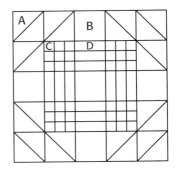

A ◿ 3⅛"   B ☐ 2¾"   C ☐ 1¼"   D ▭ 1¼" × 2¾"

JULY
26

Century of Progress
8"

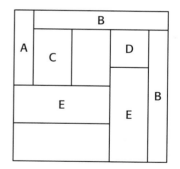

A ▢ 1½" × 4½" C ▢ 2½" × 3½" E ▢ 2½" × 5½"
B ▢ 1½" × 7½" D ▢ 2½"

JUNE
7

Doves in the Window
14"

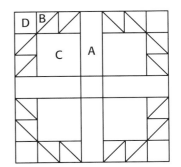

A ▭ 2½" × 6½"   B ◩ 2⅞"   C ▢ 4½"   D ▢ 2½"

Chuck-A-Luck
10"

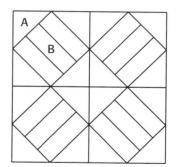

A $\square$ 3⅜" B $\square$ 1¹¹⁄₁₆" × 4¹⁄₁₆"

JUNE
8

Wandering Lover
9"

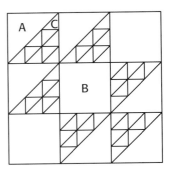

A ◻ 3⅞"   B ◻ 3½"   C ◻ 1⅞"

JULY
24

Storm Signal
8½"

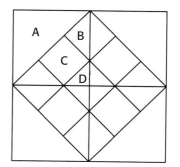

A ◻ 5⅛" B ◻ 2⅞" C ☐ 2½" D ⊠ 3¼"

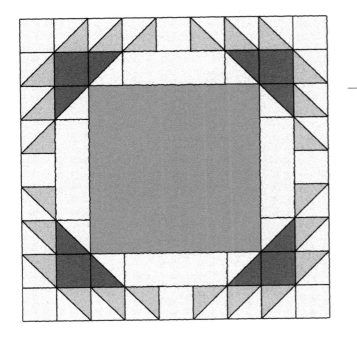

JUNE
9

Love in a Tangle
13½"

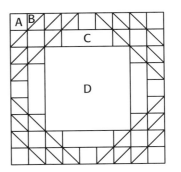

A ☐ 2"   B ◫ 2⅜"   C ☐ 2" × 5"   D ☐ 8"

JULY
23

Anchors Aweigh
8"

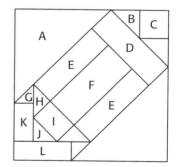

A ◩ 5⅞" D ▭ 1⅞" × 4¾" G ◩ 1⅞" J ⊠ 3"
B ◩ 2⅜" E ▭ 1¾" × 4¾" H ◩ 2⅛" K ▭ 1½" × 2½"
C ▢ 2" F ▭ 2¼" × 4¾" I ▭ 1¾" × 2¼" L ▭ 1½" × 3½"

JUNE
10

Lover's Lane
12"

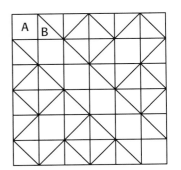

A ☐ 2½"   B ◸ 2⅞"

JULY
22

Dream Ship
10"

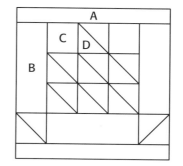

A ▭ 1½" × 10½"   B ▭ 2½" × 6½"   C ▢ 2½"   D ◩ 2⅞"

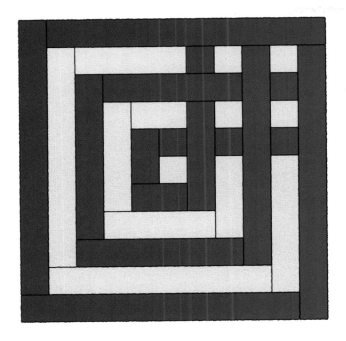

JUNE
11

True Lover's Knot
11"

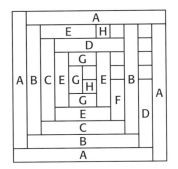

A ☐ 1½" × 10½"   C ☐ 1½" × 6½"   E ☐ 1½" × 4½"   G ☐ 1½" × 2½"

B ☐ 1½" × 8½"   D ☐ 1½" × 5½"   F ☐ 1½" × 3½"   H ☐ 1½"

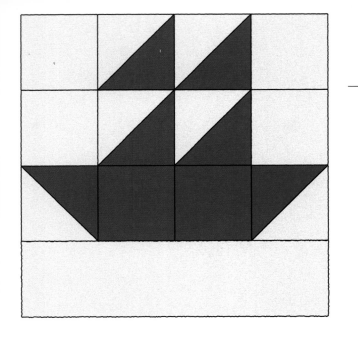

The Ship
8"

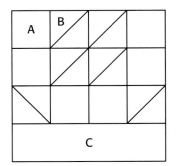

A ☐ 2½"   B ◫ 2⅞"   C ▭ 2½" × 8½"

JUNE
12

Old Maid's Puzzle
8"

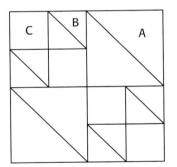

A ◻ 4⅞" B ◻ 2⅞" C ☐ 2½"

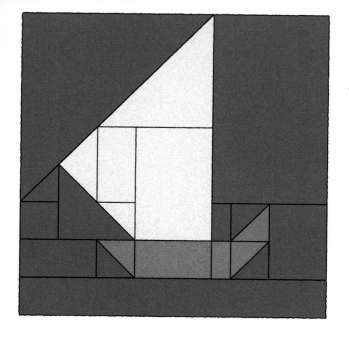

JULY
20

Dutch Sailboat
8"

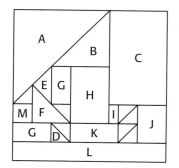

A ◿ 5⅞"

B ◿ 3⅞"

C ▭ 3½" × 5½"

D ◿ 1⅞"

E ⊠ 3¼"

F ◿ 2⅞"

G ▭ 1½" × 2½"

H ▭ 2½" × 3½"

I ▭ 1" × 1½"

J ▭ 2" × 2½"

K ▭ 1½" × 3"

L ▭ 1½" × 8½"

M ▢ 1½"

JUNE
13

Old Maid's Ramble
10"

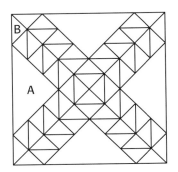

A ◻ 7¼"   B ◻ 3¼"

Ocean Waves
8"

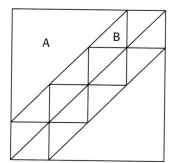

A ◿ 6⅞"   B ◿ 2⅞"

Good Luck
6"

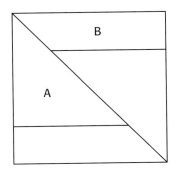

A ◻ 5⅜"   B ▭ 2" × 6½" / TT-1

Waves of the Sea
8"

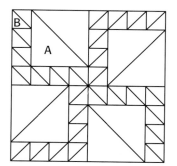

A ◹ 3⅞"   B ◹ 1⅞"

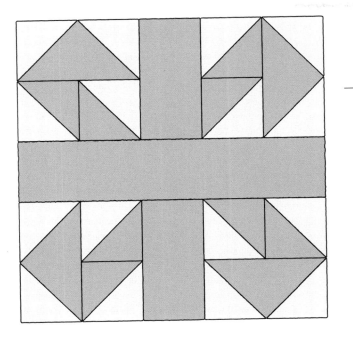

JUNE
15

Wheel of Fortune
10"

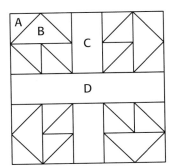

A ◱ 2⅞" B ⊠ 5¼" C ▭ 2½" × 4½" D ▭ 2½" × 10½"

JULY
17

Sailboats
6"

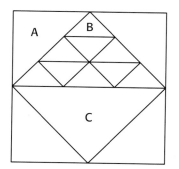

A ◸ 3⅞"   B ⊠ 3¼"   C ⊠ 7¼"

JUNE
16

Brave World
10"

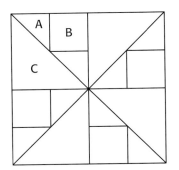

A ◻ 3⅜"   B ☐ 3"   C ◻ 5⅞"

JULY
16

Port and Starboard
8"

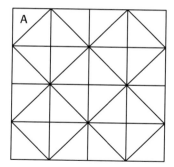

A ▱ 2⅞"

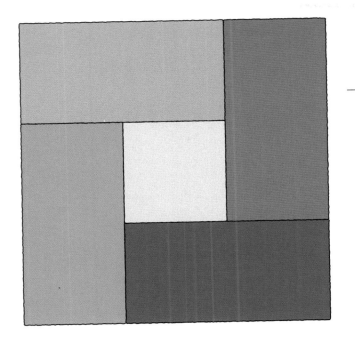

JUNE
17

Bright Hopes
9"

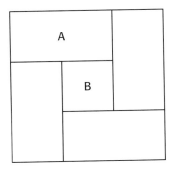

A ▭ 3½" × 6½" B ▢ 3½"

JULY
15

Lost Ship
12"

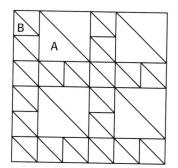

A ▱ 4⅞"   B ▱ 2⅞"

JUNE
18

Barrister's Block
12"

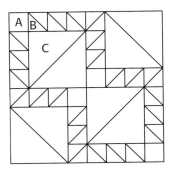

A ☐ 2" B ◩ 2⅜" C ◩ 5⅜"

JULY
14

Sailboat
8"

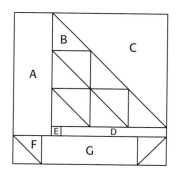

A ☐ 2½" × 7" C ◩ 6⅞" E ☐ 1" G ☐ 2" × 5½"
B ◩ 2⅞" D ☐ 1" × 6" F ◩ 2⅜"

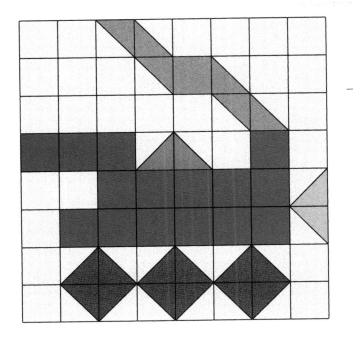

JUNE
19

Train
12"

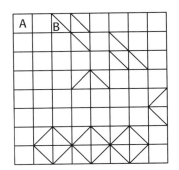

A ☐ 2"   B ◹ 2⅜"

JULY
13

Tall Ships
12"

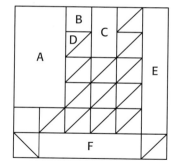

A ▢ 4½" × 8½" C ▢ 2½" × 4½" E ▢ 2½" × 10½"
B ▢ 2½" D ◩ 2⅞" F ▢ 2½" × 8½"

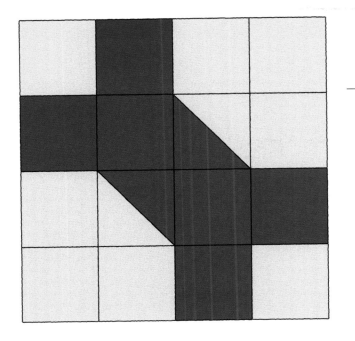

JUNE
20

Mr. Roosevelt's Necktie
8"

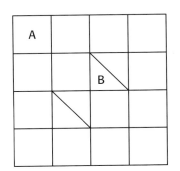

A ☐ 2½"   B ◩ 2⅞"

JULY
12

Starry Lane
12"

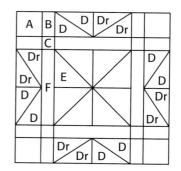

A ☐ 2½"

B ▭ 1½" × 2½"

C ☐ 1½"

D ◣ PT-5

Dr ◢ PT-5 reversed

E ◱ 3⅞"

F ▭ 1½" × 6½"

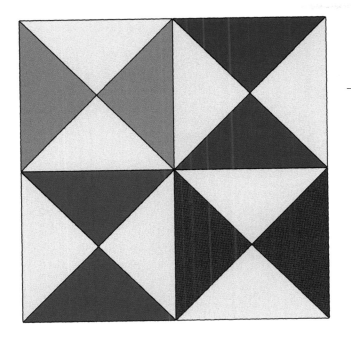

Bow Tie
6"

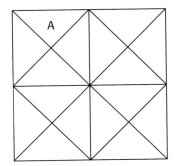

A

A ⊠ 4¼"

JULY
11

Grand Right and Left
12"

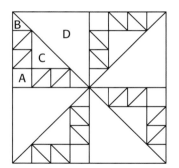

A ☐ 2"   B ◿ 2⅜"   C ◿ 3⅞"   D ◿ 6⅞"

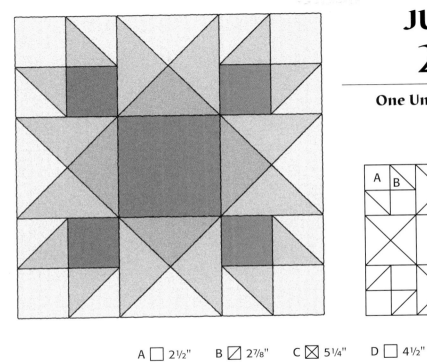

One Union Square
12"

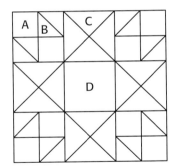

A ☐ 2½" B ◺ 2⅞" C ⊠ 5¼" D ☐ 4½"

Union Square
8"

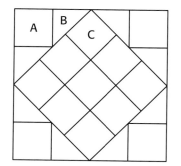

A ☐ 2½"   B ◨ 2⅞"   C ☐ 2⅜"

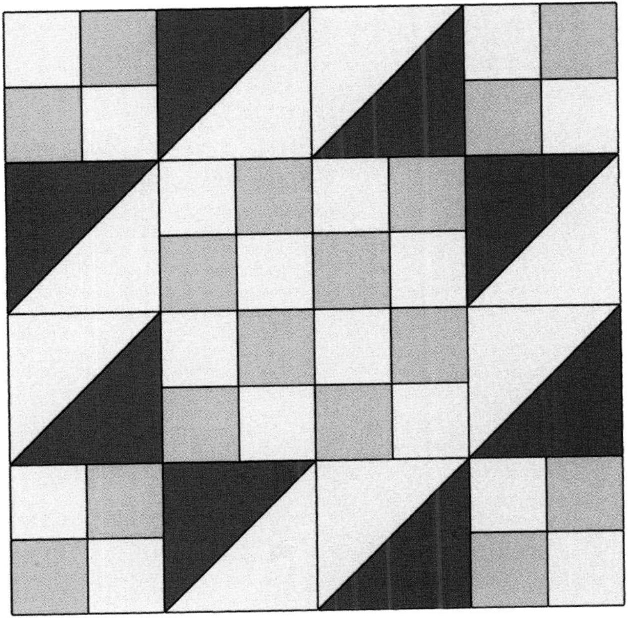

JUNE
23

Sunny Lanes
12"

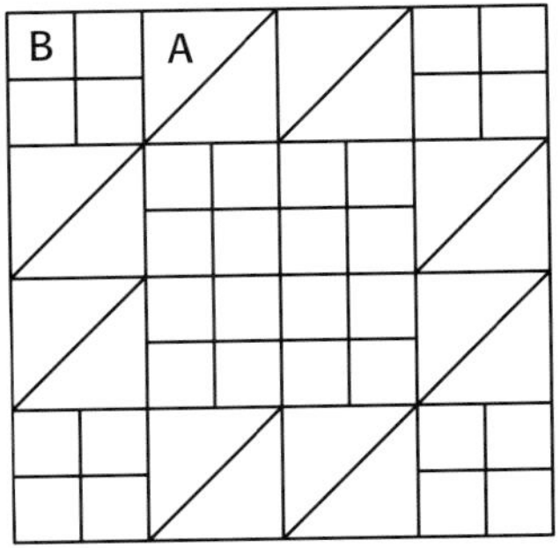

A ◪ 3⅞" B ☐ 2"

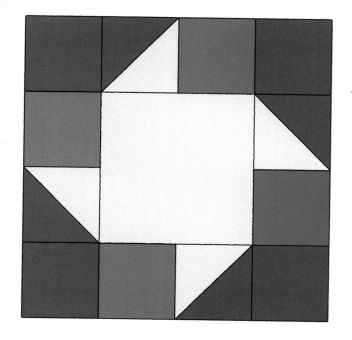

JULY
9

Paper Pinwheels
8"

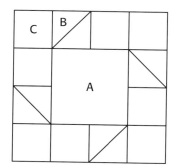

A ☐ 4½"   B ◺ 2⅞"   C ☐ 2½"

JUNE
24

World's Fair Block
12"

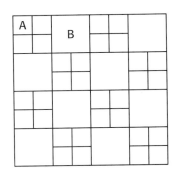

A ☐ 2"   B ☐ 3½"

JULY
8

Rolling Pinwheel
12"

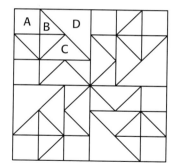

A ☐ 2½" B ◩ 2⅞" C ⊠ 5¼" D ◩ 4⅞"

JUNE
25

Odd Fellows Chain
16"

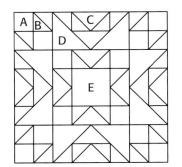

A ☐ 2½"   B ◹ 2⅞"   C ⊠ 5¼"   D ◹ 4⅞"   E ☐ 4½"

JULY
7

Yankee Puzzle
12"

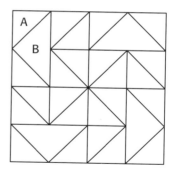

A ◻ 3⅞"   B ⊠ 7¼"

JUNE
26

Bridle Path
12"

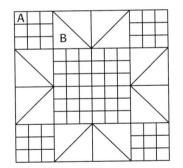

A ☐ 1½" B ◩ 3⅞"

JULY
6

Union
12"

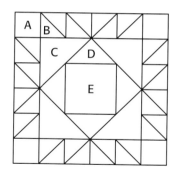

A ☐ 2½"   B ◺ 2⅞"   C ◺ 4⅞"   D ⊠ 5¼"   E ☐ 4½"

JUNE
27

State House
12"

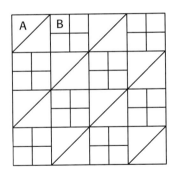

A ◹ 3⅞"   B ☐ 2"

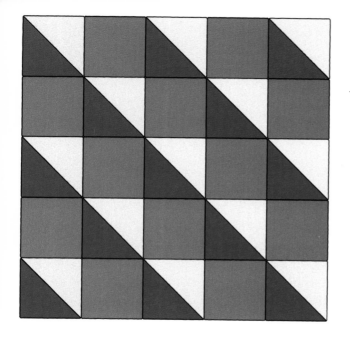

Strength in Union
10"

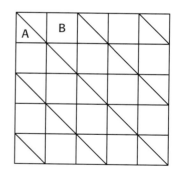

A ▱ 2⅞"   B ▢ 2½"

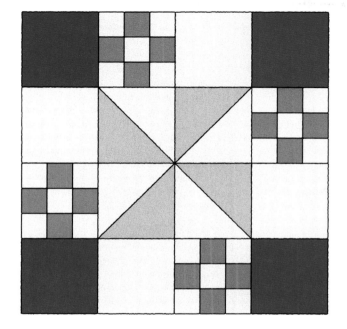

JUNE
28

White House
12"

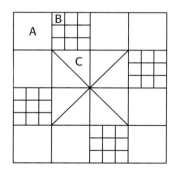

A ☐ 3½"   B ☐ 1½"   C ◹ 3⅞"

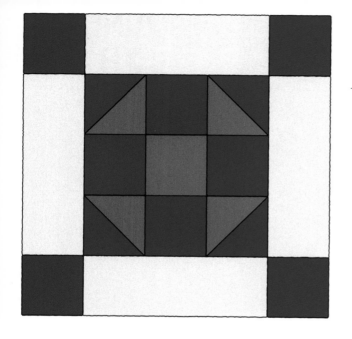

JULY
4

Philadelphia Pavement
10"

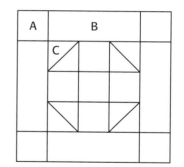

A ☐ 2½"   B ☐ 2½" × 6½"   C ◹ 2⅞"

JUNE
29

English Ivy
6"

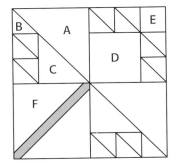

A ◻ 3⅞"   C ◻ 2⅞"   E ☐ 1½"
B ◻ 1⅞"   D ☐ 2½"   F ☐ 3½"

JULY

3

Independence Square
9"

A ☐ 2½"   B ▭ 1½" × 2½"   C ▭ 1½" × 3½"   D ☐ 1½"

JUNE
30

Summer Winds
12"

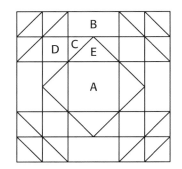

A ☐ 4½"   B ▭ 2½" × 4½"   C ◪ 2⅞"   D ☐ 2½"   E ⊠ 5¼"

JULY
2

Uncle Sam's Hourglass
12"

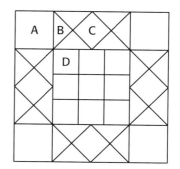

A ☐ 3½" B ☒ 4¼" C ☐ 2⅝" D ☐ 2½"

Summer
July–September

Summer starts off with a cadence of patriotic blocks celebrating Independence Day. And of course, July just wouldn't be the same without blocks made specially for the sailing season. During August, memories of life on the farm and children's favorite toys and games are featured in a variety of designs with a summertime feel. As summer vacations draw to a close and school swings back into session, choose from an assortment of schoolhouse and back-to-school blocks. September signals autumn's approach, when Flying Geese and Migrating Bird blocks are in sync with the season.

JULY
1

Stars and Stripes
12"

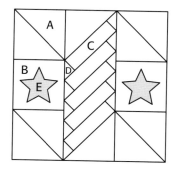

A ◻ 4⅞" B ☐ 4½" C ▭ 1⅝" × 5" D ◻ 2" E ☆ AT-6

BLOCK INDEX

A

A	Sept. 6	7½"
Aircraft	Nov. 12	12"
Airplane	Nov. 13	12"
Album	Feb. 3	9"
Album Patch	Feb. 4	15"
Almanizer	Nov. 9	12"
Alpine Cross	April 19	10"
Anchors Aweigh	July 23	8"
Angelsong	Dec. 5	5" x 6"
Anvil	Oct. 16	9"
April Tulips	April 2	16"
Arizona	April 30	12"
Arkansas Crossroads	April 27	8"
Army Star	Nov. 11	12"
Around the Corner	April 5	12"
Arrow Crown	Nov. 16	12"
Art Square	Oct. 27	8"
Aunt Dinah	Jan. 19	9"
Aunt Mary's Double Irish Chain	March 19	12"
Aunt Sukey's Choice	May 16	12"
Autumn Leaf	Oct. 3	9"
Autumn Tints	Oct. 1	10½"

B

B	Sept. 7	7½"
Bachelor's Puzzle	June 6	11¼"
Balance	Dec. 27	15"
Barbara Frietchie Star	Feb. 25	12"
Barrister's Block	June 18	12"
Baton Rouge Square	April 6	10"
Be My Valentine	Feb. 14	8"
Beacon Lights	Oct. 28	12"
Bear's Paw	Nov. 14	10½"
Beggar's Blocks	March 26	9"
Beginner's Delight	Jan. 12	10"
Best Friend	Feb. 5	14"
Bird House	May 14	6" x 10"
Bird of Paradise	March 20	12"
Birds in the Air	Sept. 19	9"
Bird's Nest	March 27	10"
BOO	Oct. 31	15"
Borrow and Lend	Jan. 30	12"
Bow Tie	June 21	6"
Brave World	June 16	10"
Bridal Wreath	June 2	6"
Bridle Path	June 26	12"
Bright Hopes	June 17	9"
Bright Star	Dec. 13	12"

Broken Dishes	March 1	10"
Brown Goose	Sept. 24	10"
Building Blocks	Aug. 17	10"
Burgoyne Surrounded	Feb. 28	15"

C

C	Sept. 8	7 ½"
Cake Stand	March 8	8"
Carrie Nation Quilt	Nov. 1	8"
Castles in the Air	Jan. 28	9"
Cat's Cradle	Aug. 21	12"
Cats and Mice	Nov. 5	12"
Century of Progress	July 26	8"
Cherry Tree	Feb. 21	7½"
Chevron	Feb. 17	9"
Children's Delight	Aug. 31	10"
Chimney Sweep	Jan. 6	10½"
Chimneys and Cornerstones	Feb. 7	8"
Chinese Puzzle	Jan. 26	10"
Chisholm Trail	Oct. 4	8"
Christmas Basket	Dec. 21	8"
Christmas Cracker	Dec. 23	8"
Christmas Tree	Dec. 3	12"
Christmas Wreath	Dec. 8	7" x 11"
Chuck-A-Luck	July 25	10"
Churn Dash	Aug. 6	7½"
City Streets	Jan. 29	9"

Clay's Choice	Feb. 26	8"
Clown	Aug. 24	10"
Coffee Cup	March 9	6" x 4"
Combination Star	Nov. 6	9"
Contrary Wife	June 4	9"
Corn and Beans	Aug. 1	12"
Corner Star	April 23	12¾"
Coronation	April 12	12"
Cotton Reels	Jan. 7	8"
Country Barn	Aug. 8	10"
Country Farm	Aug. 12	9"
Country Roads	Aug. 7	10½"
Crazy Ann	Jan. 18	10"
Creamer	March 5	6" x 3½"
Cross and Crown	April 16	10"
Cross Roads	Nov. 8	8"
Cross within a Cross	April 21	12"
Crosses and Losses	March 30	8"
Crossroads to Jericho	April 18	8"
Crown of Thorns	April 17	10"
Cups and Saucers	March 2	9"
Cut Glass Dish	March 7	12"

D

D	Sept. 9	7½"
Daffodil	May 9	8"
Darting Birds	Jan. 20	6"

Delectable Mountains	April 24	10"
Devil's Claws	April 20	12"
Dewey Dream Quilt	Oct. 20	10"
Dolley Madison's Star	Feb. 24	9"
Double Cross	Jan. 21	10"
Double Irish Chain	March 18	11"
Doves in the Window	June 7	14"
Dream Ship	July 22	10"
Duck and Ducklings	May 27	12"
Dutch Sailboat	July 20	8"
Dutchman's Puzzle	March 21	10"

E

E	Sept. 10	7½"
Economy	Jan. 15	10"
Eddystone Light	Nov. 3	9"
Eight Hands Around	Dec. 16	12"
English Ivy	June 29	6"
Evening Star	Jan. 22	9"

F

Ferris Wheel	Aug. 20	12"
Fifty-four Forty or Fight	Feb. 27	12"
Fireflies	Aug. 18	8"
Fireside Visitor	Dec. 20	9"
Flock of Geese	Sept. 22	10"
Flower Basket	May 4	10"

Flower Bud	May 5	6"
Flower Pot	May 3	10"
Flower Pot	May 13	5"
Flyfoot	July 29	8"
Flying Dutchman	Jan. 17	10"
Flying Fish	July 30	12"
Flying Geese	Sept. 20	10"
Flying Shuttles	Jan. 8	12"
Fool's Puzzle	April 1	9"
Four Corners	Jan. 25	9"
Four Knaves	Nov. 28	10"
Free Trade	Feb. 29	10"
Friendship Star	Feb. 1	6"
Friendship Star	Dec. 4	12"

G

Garden of Eden	April 13	10"
Geese in Flight	Sept. 18	12"
Gentleman's Fancy	Oct. 29	9"
Golden Gate	Oct. 8	11"
Good Luck	June 14	6"
Grand Right and Left	July 11	12"
Grandmother's Basket	May 20	10"
Grandmother's Choice	May 18	10"
Grandmother's Favorite	May 19	10"
Grape Basket	Aug. 3	10"

H

Hand of Friendship	Feb. 2	14"
Handy Andy	Jan. 13	10"
Harvest Basket	Nov. 29	10"
Hen and Chicks	May 28	10"
Here Comes Santa Claus	Dec. 9	6"
Hill and Crag	April 4	10"
Hill and Valley	July 27	9"
Hither and Yon	Oct. 21	12"
Hopscotch	Aug. 30	8"
Hour Glass	Sept. 14	9"
Hour Glass	Dec. 30	9"
House on the Hill	Sept. 2	12"
Hovering Hawks	Sept. 25	8"

I

Independence Square	July 3	9"
Indian	Nov. 18	10"
Indian Mats	Nov. 22	12"
Indian Maze	Nov. 20	12"
Indian Plume	Nov. 17	12"
Indian Squares	Nov. 21	10"
Indian Trails	Nov. 15	12"

J

Jack in the Box	Aug. 22	10"
Jack's Delight	Nov. 2	9"
Jack-O-Lantern	Oct. 30	10"
Jacob's Ladder	March 28	8"
Jefferson City	Oct. 18	9"
Johnny Round the Corner	Sept. 17	9"
Joseph's Coat	April 15	10"

K

Kansas Troubles	Feb. 8	16"
King's Crown	April 14	10"

L

Lady of the Lake	May 21	10"
Leavenworth Nine Patch	Nov. 27	10½"
Light and Shadows	Oct. 25	8"
Lighthouse	Nov. 4	10"
Lightning in the Hills	July 31	12"
Lincoln's Cabin Home	Feb. 10	9"
Lincoln's Platform	Feb. 9	10½"
Little Red Schoolhouse	Sept. 1	8"
Log Cabin	Nov. 30	9"
Log Cabin Heart	Feb. 13	4¼"
Lost Ship	July 15	12"
Love in a Tangle	June 9	13½"
Lover's Lane	June 10	12"

M

Magnolia Bud	May 10	8"
Maple Leaf	Oct. 2	9"
Market Square	Aug. 10	16"
Martha Washington Star	Feb. 23	8"
Maryland Beauty	Oct. 6	10"
May Basket	May 1	5"
May Basket	May 2	6"
Mayflower	Nov. 26	8"
Medieval Walls	Oct. 10	9"
Meeting House Square	Oct. 15	9"
Memory	May 29	12"
Memory Block	May 30	10"
Memory Wreath	May 31	12"
Menorah	Dec. 10	14" x 17"
Merry Go Round	Aug. 19	8"
Milky Way	April 11	12½"
Mineral Wells	Oct. 19	12"
Missouri Puzzle	April 10	13½"
Missouri Star	Oct. 24	8"
Mosaic	Feb. 18	8"
Mother's Choice	May 22	12"
Mother's Dream	May 24	18"
Mother's Fancy	May 25	14"
Mother's Favorite	May 23	12"
Mother's Own	May 26	8"
Mountain Homespun	Feb. 19	9"

Mr. Roosevelt's Necktie	June 20	8"
Mrs. Keller's Nine Patch	Oct. 9	10"

N

Nancy's Nosegay	May 8	8"
Nelson's Victory	Jan. 16	8"
Next Door Neighbor	Feb. 6	8"
Nine Patch Variation	Dec. 24	9"
Northumberland Star	April 28	12"
Northwind	March 11	9"

O

Ocean Waves	July 19	8"
Odd Fellows Chain	June 25	16"
Oklahoma Boomer	Jan. 31	6"
Old-Fashioned Fruit Basket	Aug. 2	12"
Old Favorite	Jan. 24	12"
Old Home	Sept. 3	11"
Old Maid's Puzzle	June 12	8"
Old Maid's Ramble	June 13	10"
One Union Square	June 22	12"
Our Village Green	Aug. 11	10"
Overall Bill	Aug. 14	4"
Ozark Trail	Oct. 7	10"

P

Block	Date	Size
Paper Pinwheels	July 9	8"
Path Through the Woods	Aug. 15	10"
Paths and Stiles	Aug. 9	9"
Peace and Plenty	Nov. 24	9"
Philadelphia Pavement	July 4	10"
Pine Tree	Dec. 1	10"
Plaid	Sept. 15	10"
Port and Starboard	July 16	8"
Pot of Flowers	May 7	10"
Prairie Queen	April 22	9"
Premium Star	Sept. 29	10"
Prickly Pear	Aug. 4	10½"
Proud Pine	Dec. 11	12"
Providence	Dec. 26	10"
Puss in a Corner	Jan. 23	7½"
Puss in the Corner	Dec. 15	12"

Q

Block	Date	Size
Queen Victoria's Crown	Oct. 17	13⅛"
Queen's Crown	Sept. 28	10"
Queen's Petticoat	Sept. 12	9"

R

Block	Date	Size
Rail Fence	Feb. 12	12"
Rambler	Jan. 14	10"
Resolutions	Dec. 29	13½"
Ribbon Block	Dec. 6	14"
Rising Star	Dec. 22	12"
Road to Oklahoma	March 23	8"
Rocking Horse	Aug. 26	10½"
Rocky Road	March 24	9"
Rolling Pinwheel	July 8	12"
Rosebud	May 6	9"

S

Block	Date	Size
Sailboat	July 14	8"
Sailboats	July 17	6"
Salt Lake City	April 7	12"
Sargeant's Chevron	Nov. 10	8"
School Boy	Sept. 5	8" x 12"
School Girl	Sept. 4	8" x 12"
School Girl's Puzzle	Aug. 28	10"
Schoolhouse	Sept. 11	12"
Seesaw	Aug. 23	8"
Sew and Sew	Jan. 11	10" x 12"
Shamrock	March 17	9"
Ship, The	July 21	8"
Shoo Fly	Aug. 16	9"
Silent Star	Dec. 19	9"
Single Irish Chain	March 16	10"
Sister's Choice	May 17	10"
Snail's Trail	March 31	12"
Snow Crystals	Jan. 4	16"
Snowball	Jan. 1	6"

Snowflake	Jan. 2	12"
Snowy Windows	Jan. 3	8"
Southern Belle	April 25	10"
Spider	Oct. 12	9"
Spider's Den	Oct. 13	12"
Spinning Arrows	Nov. 23	12"
Spinning Tops	Aug. 29	10"
Spool and Bobbin	Jan. 9	8"
Spool of Thread	Jan. 10	8"
Spools	Jan. 5	6"
Spring Has Come	March 22	12"
Square and Star	March 29	12"
Squares Upon Squares	Nov. 7	10"
Squash Blossom	Sept. 27	12"
Star-Crossed Christmas	Dec. 7	13½"
Star of Bethlehem	Dec. 25	12"
Star of Hope	Dec. 17	9"
Starry Lane	July 12	12"
Starry Path	Dec. 18	10"
Star and Pinwheel	Oct. 23	12"
Stars and Stripes	July 1	12"
State House	June 27	12"
Steps to the Altar	June 5	12"
Storm Signal	July 24	8½"
Strength in Union	July 5	10"
Sugar Bowl	March 6	4" x 3½"
Summer Winds	June 30	12"
Sun and Shade	July 28	15"
Sunbonnet Sue	Aug. 13	4"
Sunny Lanes	June 23	12"
Sunshine	April 3	16"
Swamp Angel	April 26	12"
Swing in the Center	Aug. 25	9"

T

Table for Four	Oct. 14	11"
Tail of Benjamin's Kite	March 15	9"
Tall Ships	July 13	12"
Tea for Four	March 10	12"
Tea Leaf	Oct. 11	9"
Teacup	March 4	5" x 3½"
Teapot	March 3	11" x 6"
Telephone	Jan. 27	12"
Tennessee Pine	Dec. 12	12"
Texas Puzzle	Sept. 30	9"
Texas Treasure	Feb. 20	12"
Three Steps	Dec. 28	12"
Thunder and Lightning	Sept. 16	12"
Towers of Camelot	Sept. 13	9"
Train	June 19	12"
Tree of Life	Dec. 2	12"
Triangle Weave	Oct. 5	8"
True Lover's Knot	Feb. 16	14"
True Lover's Knot	June 11	11"

Tulip	May 12	8" x 10"
Tulip Time	May 11	8" x 12"
Turkey Tracks	Nov. 25	9"
Twinkling Star	Dec. 14	12"
Twister	April 8	10"

U

Uncle Sam's Hourglass	July 2	12"
Underground Railroad	Feb. 11	12"
Union	July 6	12"
Union Square	July 10	8"

V

Vase of Flowers	March 25	12"
Vermont	April 9	12"

W

Wampum	Nov. 19	9"
Wandering Lover	June 8	9"
Washington's Elm	Feb. 22	16"
Watercolor Heart	Feb. 15	6"
Watering Can	May 15	11"
Waterwheel	Aug. 5	7"
Waves of the Sea	July 18	8"
Weathervane	March 12	12"
Wedding March	June 3	18"
Wedding Ring	June 1	10"

Wheel of Fortune	June 15	10"
Wheel of Time	Oct. 22	10"
Whirligig	Aug. 27	8"
Whirling Square	Oct. 26	8"
White House	June 28	12"
Wild Duck	Sept. 26	8"
Wild Goose Chase	Sept. 21	10"
Windmill	March 13	10"
Windmill Square	March 14	8"
Winged Square	Sept. 23	12"
World's Fair Block	June 24	12"
Wyoming Valley Star	April 29	15"

Y

Yankee Puzzle	July 7	12"
Year's Favorite	Dec. 31	8"